The Farmstead Egg Guide & Cookbook

The Farmstead Egg Guide & Cookbook

Terry Golson

Photography by Ben Fink

Houghton Mifflin Harcourt

Boston • New York • 2014

For information about permission to reproduce selections
from this book, write to Permissions, Houghton Mifflin Harcourt
Publishing Company, 215 Park Avenue South, New York,
New York 10003.

www.hmhco.com

Library of Congress Cataloging-in-Publication Data

Golson, Terry Blonder. Farmstead egg guide and cookbook /
Terry Blonder Golson ; photography by Ben Fink.
     p. cm.
Includes bibliographical references and index.
ISBN 978-1-118-62795-2 (pbk.); 978-0-544-18840-2 (ebk.)
1. Cooking (Eggs) 2. Poultry farms. 3. Egg gathering. I. Title.
TX745.G647 2013
641.6'75—dc23
                    2013027719

Printed in the United States of America
DOC 10 9 8 7 6 5 4 3 2 1

To my husband, Steve.

Acknowledgements

When a book is published there are always so many people to thank—a few I know well, others only through email, and still others contribute without us ever being in direct contact. I am most grateful to every one of them. I've known my editor, Linda Ingroia, for many years, but we've never worked on a book together. I'm indebted to her for wanting to do this project and for shepherding *The Farmstead Egg Guide & Cookbook* through the publishing process, and keeping it on schedule, despite formidable obstacles that included a hurricane, flooding, and power outages. Thanks, too, to my agent, Carrie Hannigan, who worked diligently to make this book happen. I'm indebted to Ben Fink for his photographs. They are not only gorgeous, but they have heart and soul and convey exactly how I feel about my cooking, my hens, and my home. Speaking of home, that is where all of my writing begins, and it is nurtured, embraced, and made joyful because of my husband and sons. Thank you, all.

CONTENTS

COPYRIGHT BY
RELIABLE POULTRY JOURNAL

The Recipes

Introduction

Almost two decades ago a neighbor gave me one sweet little fluffy-feathered older hen. Buk-Buk was the last of my friend's chickens left over from her daughter's 4-H project. Buk-Buk and her ramshackle coop appeared in my life at a time when I had a toddler and worked as a food writer. I had a degree in animal science that I wasn't using in my career, but I still had a hankering for farm animals. I couldn't fit horses or goats into my suburban backyard, but I had thought that someday it would be fun to have a flock of laying hens, and so was happy that Buk-Buk gave me the excuse to get started. I didn't know much about chickens, but I did recognize that they are social animals and need chicken friends. I soon got Buk-Buk a companion hen, and then "the girls" needed a larger coop. The new spacious housing could accommodate more chickens. Which I got. I haven't been without a flock of hens in my backyard and fresh eggs in the refrigerator since.

Over the years I wrote a couple of cookbooks and many newspaper and magazine articles. I exhaustively tested recipes. It soon became clear that the dishes made with eggs from my own hens were markedly different when compared to those prepared with supermarket eggs. In fact, when developing a newspaper recipe, I actually went out and bought commercial eggs so that I could be confident that the recipes would work for the majority of my readers, who used the poorer quality of egg found in the market. In 2006, when I wrote *The Farmstead Egg Cookbook*, I was finally able to focus entirely on good eggs from backyard hens. I am so pleased to be able to bring this book back into print in this expanded edition.

If you buy eggs at the farmers' market or are able to purchase a carton from a neighbor, this book will help you to make the best of them. Perhaps those eggs have you thinking that you want a flock of your own.

When I started keeping a small flock of hens in my pretty yard, it was unusual. Most people thought that only "real" farmers raised chicken for eggs. Incorporating a domestic farm animal (even one as small as a chicken) into a typical suburban backyard just wasn't done. But recently, small-scale chicken keeping has seen a resurgence. It's even become stylish! It's also become easy to do. Caring for chickens requires some specialized equipment and feed, which used to be inaccessible to anyone who didn't have a feed store in their neighborhood. But now, even people in urban areas can find everything they need online. Prefab coops are available at box stores and high-end retailers. Suburban pet stores are even stocking chicken feed!

However, chicken keeping isn't for everyone. This new edition has information to help you decide whether having chickens in your backyard is right for you, and what to do to get started. Throughout *The Farmstead Egg Guide & Cookbook*, I share my many years of experience. If you live in a place that doesn't allow chickens, or if it's just not feasible for you right now, then you are welcome to vicariously enjoy the charms of my flock. You can watch my hens on live-streaming cams at my website, HenCam.com.

A Note on Ingredients

EGGS: All of the recipes were tested with fresh eggs from my hens, the size of which varies. A standard supermarket "large" egg is 2 ounces, and so for the greatest ease of use I specify that size in the recipes.

SALT: For daily cooking, I use kosher salt. I think that the flavor is cleaner than the other widely available salts sold for cooking. When adding salt to a meal at the table, I use a good-quality sea salt. There are many available; the differences between them can be nuanced or dramatic. It's worth trying several and finding your own favorite.

DAIRY PRODUCTS: I think that there is a marked difference between brands of milk and other dairy products. For example, a large dairy's whole milk tastes far sweeter than a local farm's product. When I can, I buy local. I'm fussy about the yogurt that I purchase, too, as texture and tartness is unique to each brand. Many dairy products are regional, and so you'll have to taste for yourself. You'll notice a change for the better in your recipes when the basic ingredients are the best that they can be.

MEAT: Just as conscientiously and lovingly raised eggs taste better and are better for you, so too are meats raised on small farms. I try to buy all of the meat that I cook for my family from local farmers who do right by the animals and the land. The cows and pigs are raised on pasture. When it is time for harvest, they are trucked a short distance to a small slaughterhouse. Stresses are minimized. This comes through in the quality and flavor of the products. An added benefit is that my support of these farmers enables the farms, and their beautiful pastoral land-scapes, to survive—a benefit for all. Not everyone has access to such good food, but if you can find it, it is well worth purchasing. It is more expensive, but I serve smaller portions and make recipes that use a smaller amount to greater effect.

Raising Chickens, Cultivating Farmstead Eggs

About Eggs and Egg Laying

Supermarket eggs are so commonplace that we take them for granted. All of the eggs at the market look the same. Outside they're perfectly smooth, and are uniform in shape and color. Inside, they all look and taste the same. It's a stretch to even imagine that chickens produced them. It's not until you begin collecting eggs from backyard hens that you realize how special and unique eggs can be. Because there are differences, even among commercial eggs, I've created a purchasing guide here. You'll also learn more about how eggs are produced and how best to store and handle them.

Eggs in the Marketplace

If you don't have your own hens (or if yours aren't laying because they're broody, or because it's winter, or because of any number of other reasons), you will have to go out and purchase a dozen eggs. The choices can be bewildering. There are almost no regulations defining types of eggs; some of the information on the cartons is misleading, and interpreting the freshness date can require a calculator.

The first thing to understand is that regulation of the laying hen industry is piecemeal and that there are various state and federal agencies that have a say in one part or another. Packaging and inspection of facilities vary by state. United States Department of Agriculture grades have nothing to do with how the hens are housed, raised, or fed. The USDA system of sizing and grading eggs began in the early twentieth century as a marketing tool to gain consumer confidence when eggs went from being a local product to being one shipped nationwide in refrigerated trucks from warehouses. USDA grades and sizing remain a marketing tool, which is in fact paid for by the egg producers. This grading system is not mandatory. USDA egg grades simply specify size and a level of freshness when packed—but not the freshness of the eggs once they reach the market. Eggs are graded at a processing plant, and by federal law eggs can be packed and shipped up to 30 days after laying, so it can be weeks before they are sold to consumers. Knowing how old the carton of eggs is that you put into your shopping cart is not always obvious. Stamping a date on the package is not required by the USDA; some states have labeling laws, but others don't. Sometimes an egg company will stamp a carton with the Julian date (instead of months, this system goes by numerical day; for example, February 5 is 36.) Other producers stamp with "sell by," "expiration," or "use by." "Use by" can be a date up to three months after the eggs were laid.

What follows are general classifications of eggs for sale:

Inexpensive Eggs at Supermarkets and Convenience Stores

The vast majority of eggs sold through supermarkets come from gigantic egg production facilities (sometimes called CAFOs or factory farms). "Farm fresh" on the carton, and a picture of a barn, sunshine, and a hen on grass, do not reflect the actual circumstances that these eggs come from. Barns filled with tens of thousands of chickens in battery cages are the norm. Be skeptical of "humane seals of approval." The egg industry, under the guise of the United Egg Producers, marks cartons with their own stamp. Read their standards online and you'll see that they support beak burning, severe crowding, and other inhumane practices. Even if animal rights aren't important to you, what goes into the eggs probably is. The USDA prohibits the feeding of hormones but does allow antibiotics in the daily ration. This sub-therapeutic use of drugs (for growth, not to treat a specific disease) is linked to "superbugs"—diseases that humans get that we can no longer treat because the bacteria have become resistant to antibiotics.

Also, caged hens are fed the least expensive ration that still allows for high egg production. Egg flavor has much to do with the lifestyle and diet of the hen. That's one reason why inexpensive supermarket eggs are pale imitators of good farmstead eggs. My own personal choice is that if the standard supermarket egg is the only type available, I do without.

Eggs from Free-Range or Cage-Free Hens

The federal government does not regulate the terms "free-range" and "cage-free" when they are applied to egg-laying poultry. Usually all that these terms mean is that the hens aren't kept in wire cages. Many cage-free hens are crowded wing to wing in large barns and never see sunlight or breathe fresh air. Consumers are demanding change, and more and more factory farms are switching to cage-free facilities. Although this is a step up from the cages, the conditions that these birds are kept in are far different from the bucolic image often represented on the egg cartons. Those packages, too, often have various "humane society" stamps of approval. Some of these marks have more meaning than others, and

it is worth going online and reading the organization's fine print rather than making a decision based on the packaging.

"Nutritional" Eggs

Some commercial producers claim that their eggs are higher in nutrients such as omega-3 fatty acids, or are lower in cholesterol, or have lots of vitamin E. By adjusting the feed, these "nutritional" eggs can be created. For example, to get the omega-3 count up, flaxseed is added to the hens' diet. They do this because the bulk of the hens' ration is poor-quality feed, often bakery by-products and cheap grains. On the other hand, the ration fed to backyard chickens, the laying hen pellets bought in bags at feed stores, is usually of a much higher quality. Farmstead hens also get to eat a variety of foods, including greens and insects, and so don't need supplements in order for their eggs to be full of good nutrients. (This has been confirmed in laboratory comparisons of eggs.)

After doing my own taste tests, I've found that the flavor of the "nutritional" eggs is the same as that of the regular commercial eggs, and nothing like the eggs from my own hens. Despite the added nutrients, these supermarket eggs are bland. The eggs from my hens have a robust, eggy flavor.

Organic Eggs

Both federal and state governments regulate the term "organic." Organic eggs come from hens fed vegetarian, organic feed. Feed affects the color, flavor, and nutrient content of eggs. It also affects cost. Farmers pay a premium for high-quality feed. Since the flavor of the grain goes right through to the eggs, you might decide that the expense is worth it. Organic eggs cannot come from caged hens; however they do not necessarily come from hens that ever step foot outside of huge buildings crowded with other hens. This is a case where you have to know your grower. Cornucopia, an organization fighting to keep the meaning in the term "organic," has a list online (cornucopia.org) of all organic egg producers. Cornucopia has graded their facilities. It's eye-opening to see the wide range of farming systems that can fall under the "organic" moniker. It's worth seeking out eggs that Cornucopia ranks as best.

Pastured Eggs

Although the term "pastured" isn't regulated, it is generally understood to mean that the flock is outside all day and only goes inside to lay eggs and to roost at night. Some farmers use electric net fencing and moveable coops so that the hens are frequently given access to fresh fields. On other farms, the hens may be kept in a permanent yard but are able to move about freely, scratch in the dirt, and hunt for bugs and other tidbits. If I have to buy eggs, buying from a farmer who pastures the hens is my first choice. However, that's still no guarantee that the eggs are fresh. The larger farms will likely wash their eggs, sort by size, and refrigerate before sale. They should mark the laying date on the cartons. If buying at a farmers' market, from a cooler at the bottom of a driveway, or from a neighbor, don't hesitate to ask how old the eggs are, about the lives of the chickens, and about how the eggs have been handled.

Brown, White, and Blue-Green Eggs

The color of the eggshell has nothing to do with quality or flavor. Different breeds of hens lay different colors of eggs. Inside they are all the same.

Despite that, in some regions consumers prefer white eggs, and in other locales people prefer brown. This is a holdover from the early twentieth century, when farmers in different regions had distinct breed preferences. Farmers in the South, and later in California, kept Leghorns, a breed that does well in heat and humidity. They lay white eggs. Farmers in the North and the Midwest preferred winter-hardy breeds, with thick feather coats and small combs, that thrived in freezing temperatures. These hens usually lay brown eggs. If a housewife saw a white egg in a market in New England, she'd know that it had been shipped a far distance and was probably old. A buyer in the South would be equally wary of a brown egg. Even now, with fast refrigerated transport, these regional preferences for eggshell color remain.

Today, most eggs offered for sale are usually either brown or white, but there are others to be had. Old-fashioned breeds lay a spectrum of colors, from olive green to bright blue, from white to chocolate brown, from beige to speckled. With the advent of factory farming, those beautiful eggs and the hens that laid them almost died out. However, nowadays, with the resurgence of backyard chicken keeping, there has also been a resurgence of these heritage breeds. Some small farmers are finding that those chickens are better suited to a life on pasture. Other growers are finding that consumers are willing to pay more for a pretty blue egg. Those of us with backyard flocks often select which breeds we keep with an eye on a varied egg basket. Just keep in mind that beauty is only shell deep and that the contents are the same!

Farmstead Eggs: Eggs from Your Own Hens

Farmstead eggs come from small flocks of content hens. All of us with backyard coops have a slightly different way of doing things. Some urban chickens have little space to roam; their country cousins might have woods and meadows. Some hens are fed organic feed; others get commercial laying hen pellets. Some get the weeds from a garden, while others have cabbages bought for them from the supermarket. But regardless of your setup, the best things about eggs from your own hens is that you know what your hens are eating and that you know exactly how fresh your eggs are. As I'll talk about later, freshness matters. I also believe that the quality of an egg laid by a happy backyard hen is far superior to that of the eggs from caged hens. I write more about this in the section on page 19.

There are also the intangible benefits of collecting eggs from your own hens. Chickens raised in commercial henhouses are skittish and stressed when someone enters their barn. Farmstead hens are happy to see people. My girls are brazenly forward. When a visitor comes within sight, they dash up to the fence and cluck loudly, as if to say, "What do you have for me?" It is a gift to have these animals in my life, producing such good food. Each egg that each hen lays is appreciated.

Are Farmstead Eggs Nutritionally Better?

There is much debate as to whether organic and farmstead eggs have any nutritional value over the eggs from caged hens. Some studies have shown a marked difference, but others have not. Companies that offer eggs "high in omega fatty acids" alter the nutritional value of their eggs by tweaking ingredients in the feed, and so it makes sense that the eggs from my hens, roaming the meadow and eating a varied diet, would also benefit from the good foods that they consume. Certainly the eggs that I collect are high in carotenoids, as is seen by the eggs' dark yellow yolks. Carotenoids are pigments that are found in red, yellow, and orange vegetables. They are potent antioxidants, thought to be essential for one's health because, among other actions, they protect the body from aging and macular degeneration. Carotenoids are a reason that nutritionists encourage the consumption of dark green leafy vegetables and orange squash. Those same compounds can be found in eggs with sunny yellow yolks. Commercial farmers might feed chemicals to create yellow yolks, but I know that the sunny yellow centers of the eggs from my hens are there because of the natural foods that they eat. Even if the eggs from my hens had the same nutritional profile as commercial eggs, I'd still think them better, as they are from chickens living in a healthy environment, eating a healthy and varied diet.

One very important difference between eggs from a small flock and supermarket eggs (even organic eggs) is how they are handled after laying. With few exceptions, hens raised in commercial facilities are crowded, whether "cage-free" or not. The environment is filled with feces, insects, and vermin, which contaminate the shells, and so the eggs must be cleaned. All commercial eggs are put through a hot water bath laced with sanitizers. Usually this is a chlorine wash. Organic eggs are cleaned with approved chemicals, but chemicals nonetheless. Even if only trace amounts remain on the egg, it affects the quality. Eggshells are porous and over

time take on the smells of the air around them. I've been in storage rooms at egg processing plants. The air made my eyes water. (I've written more about the downside of eggs going through hot water baths in the section on egg safety.) But farmstead eggs aren't laid in such conditions. Most of the eggs that I collect don't need any washing. They are perfectly clean. On the rare occasion that a hen has stepped a muddy foot on an egg, or there's a bit of manure stuck to the shell, all I have to do is to wipe it with a damp paper towel.

Sizes and Shapes of Eggs

USDA egg sizes are the recognized standard. For a whole egg in its shell, these are:

Small	1½ ounces
Medium	1¾ ounces
Large	2 ounces
Extra-large	2¼ ounces
Jumbo	2½ ounces

When you buy a carton of eggs at the supermarket, they are all the same size and shape. But farmstead eggs come in as many sizes as there are breeds of chickens. My petite White Leghorn, Betsy, lays eggs that are barely over 1 ounce. Opal, my Delaware hen, lays eggs that top the chart at almost 3 ounces. Not only that, but egg size changes with the calendar. In midsummer my hens lay their largest eggs, but as the laying season comes to a close in the fall, the eggs become smaller. The age of the hen matters, too. A pullet (a young hen) will lay her first egg when she is somewhere between 17 and 24 weeks of age. It takes a while for her reproductive system to get into sync. Sometimes her first egg is so tiny that it is smaller than a robin's egg. Called a "wind egg," it's often yolkless. (Wind eggs are adorable, and if you find one you'll want to save it. I keep mine set aside in a decorative bowl. Just leave it out and it will dry and last forever.) But soon enough, the hens' reproductive systems get in gear and their eggs form correctly. For the first month or so, the eggs will be a tad small, and then gradually they will get larger.

In a backyard flock you'll notice that each hen lays an egg of a distinctive size and shape. Some chickens lay eggs that are pointy on each end, some lay eggs that are rounded. I have a hen that lays a narrow egg, and another girl lays one that is bulbous. This can surprise the first-time hen keeper, as supermarket eggs all look identical. That's because the chickens that lay them are genetically closely related, and because any egg that doesn't fit the strict norm is sorted out and sold in a liquid egg product, not in the shell. Personally, I think that the variety in farmstead eggs is one of the benefits of keeping hens. I can identify which hens laid which eggs and say a silent "thank you" to them as I cook.

Certainly cooking with supermarket eggs makes following a recipe easy. "Two large eggs" are always two eggs. But if you have a carton of farmstead eggs, they might come from chickens of different sizes, and so their eggs will be different sizes, too. Chickens can be divided into two classifications: large birds and bantams. A standard large chicken is probably what you imagine when you think of a hen. A Rhode Island Red is a classic-looking laying hen. She weighs about 6½ pounds. Her egg will weigh about 2 ounces. Some breeds are much larger than that. A Brahma can weigh more than 9 pounds. Her eggs would fit into a jumbo carton. On the other end of the spectrum are the bantams, which, even when fully grown, weigh no more than 2 pounds. Their eggs weigh barely more than 1 ounce. When I collect eggs from my flock, I find eggs that range from 1½ ounces (from my bantam White Leghorn Betsy) to almost 3 ounces (from my Delaware, Opal). When a recipe calls for an egg, what it is really asking for is a 2-ounce egg. Obviously, the eggs in my basket don't always fit that parameter.

In this book, all of my recipes are based on a 2-ounce egg, often called "large" on cartons and in cookbooks. Using the exact volume quantity isn't essential for recipes like scrambled eggs, but in many dishes, like custards, the proportion of the ingredients has to be exact for the recipe to work. Because of this, I keep a small digital scale on my counter. I weigh the eggs of various sizes until they add up to what would be the standard weight. For example, if I need four eggs, that would be 8 ounces.

There is another issue when comparing commercial eggs to farmstead eggs, and that is the proportion of yolk to white. As a general rule, one large egg is about ¼ cup of volume. One yolk is just over 1 tablespoon, and one white is just less than 3 tablespoons. A large egg contains a yolk that weighs about ½ ounce (33 percent of the liquid weight of the egg). But this proportion does not stay constant as the size of the egg changes. Jumbo eggs have a smaller proportion of yolk to white than do smaller eggs. The opposite is true for small eggs, which can be up to 44 percent yolk. A yolk from Betsy is almost the same size as one from Edwina, my large Barred Plymouth Rock! A higher proportion of yolk can make a pronounced difference in a recipe. For example, an omelet made from all small eggs will taste intensely of yolks. A pound cake made with small eggs will be denser and softer than a cake made from extra-large eggs. Rather than this variety being an annoyance in the kitchen, I see it as one of the joys of having farmstead eggs. Selecting the right egg for the recipe, and knowing which hen made that egg, connects me to the foods that I feed my family.

The Farmstead Egg Quality Difference

I've done blind taste tests of every brand of egg at the supermarket and specialty store. I've hard-cooked eggs from organic growers and from small local flocks. Every test clearly shows a marked difference between commercial and farmstead eggs. Standard eggs taste faintly metallic, and the yolks have a pallid color and a correspondingly bland flavor. Cage-free eggs vary and sometimes have dark yolks, but usually their flavor is little better than that of standard eggs. But yolks from farmstead eggs are usually a brilliant sunflower yellow and have an intense yolky flavor. Whites from farmstead eggs also have outstanding qualities. They taste clean, with none of the off flavors found in standard eggs.

The USDA grades eggs according to freshness and certain visual criteria. Although the standard for Grade A specifies a "clear" and "viscous" white, in my comparisons that supermarket egg doesn't look anything like a farmstead egg. A farmstead egg has a thick and shimmering white that is faintly opaque. Supermarket egg whites are thin and almost clear when raw.

This difference in the whites is not simply aesthetic—it very much affects the cooking properties of the eggs. Thin, pallid whites spread out 5½ inches or more when cooked, and often the yolk breaks. But when I crack an egg freshly collected from my coop into a frying pan, it will spread out into a compact

4-inch circle with a yolk that stands tall and whole in the center. This makes a difference with a simple fried egg, but it also matters in any recipe where the whites provide structure and lightness, such as in an angel food cake, a soufflé, or a meringue.

There are a number of reasons for this marked difference between farmstead eggs and all others. The first is freshness. Eggs are perishable. As soon as it is laid, an egg begins to deteriorate. The water inside the egg evaporates and the contents shrink. Odors from outside the egg are absorbed. The membranes that hold the egg together separate. The yolk flattens. An egg starts out with two distinct whites, but those will meld into one and become thin with time. Yolks are the perfect medium for bacterial growth, and if the egg is kept warm and moist, the bacteria will multiply. That all sounds dire, but if handled properly, this is a very slow process and the egg will remain usable for many weeks. Farmstead eggs, collected soon after laying and stored immediately in the refrigerator, stay far fresher than commercial eggs that are washed in hot (100°F) sanitizing washes and then take hours, if not days, to cool. Farmstead eggs go right from your refrigerator to your kitchen counter. Commercial eggs travel from farm to processor to warehouse to supermarket. Even if they start out as Grade A, there are many steps along the way that can prove detrimental.

Even if the eggs at the supermarket were as fresh as farmstead eggs, there would still be differences between them. When chickens are living in stressful environments, the quality of their eggs is affected. The most obvious sign of stress is thin shells, which crack easily. Commercial growers have losses due to breakage. You'll notice how sturdy the shells from your young hens are. Stress has other impacts, too. My backyard chickens are content, but hens housed with 50,000 others, without sunlight, dust baths, and space to roam, are not. Studies show that stressed hens lay eggs with more blood spots. Blood spots are formed when the yolk is released from the oviduct. Eggs with blood spots are edible but unsightly. You might never see a blood spot until you have your own hens, and because of that it might seem as though backyard eggs have more of them. However, the truth is that the big processors use sensors to detect these spots and divert those eggs from being put into cartons. Commercial facilities see great losses from blood spots.

The quality of the feed also makes a difference in the quality of the eggs. Chickens in the huge commercial facilities eat a ration carefully designed to give them the fat, protein, and minerals they need to lay eggs, but the producers want to feed them for as low a cost as possible. Ingredients in the factory-farmed hen's ration include bakery by-products and meat and bone meal (not human grade). Farmstead chickens also get commercial feed in the form of laying hen pellets, but of a much higher quality. I buy a vegetarian feed so that there are no questionable meat by-products. Backyard and farmstead hens eat a varied diet beyond the grains in the pellets. Mine also get greens from the yard and garden. In the winter I hang cabbages for them to peck. (See more about feeding hens on page 40.) The varied, nutritious, and wholesome food that farmstead hens eat is reflected in the quality of their eggs. Commercial hens are fed chemicals to create a yellow yolk; my hens have deep orange yolks because of the nutrient-dense whole foods that they consume. In the fall, I feed the girls leftover jack-o'-lanterns, which makes their egg yolks a warm, rich orange. In the spring, when they peck at clover, the yolks are a buttery yellow. Not only are their eggs beautiful, but they also taste eggier than pale supermarket eggs. Once you've had a farmstead egg, simply scrambled up in a pan with a touch of butter, there will be no doubt in your mind of how good they are.

How an Egg Is Made (and Why They Don't All Look the Same)

A dozen eggs bought at the supermarket all look the same, smooth and identical in shape and color; the hens that make them all look alike too, and are closely related genetically. These hens are designed to lay a uniform product. Eggs that deviate from the norm are sorted out by machines and don't end up in cartons. In contrast, the eggs from our own back-yard hens are a varied lot, which is no surprise since farmstead chickens are usually a many hued, vari-ously sized motley group. The eggs in our baskets are as unique as the birds that lay them.

On the most basic level, breed determines the color and size of the egg. You can try to select your backyard hens with an eye to what your egg basket will look like, but it doesn't always go as planned. I got a Welsummer because that breed is known to lay dark brown eggs. My Welsummer, named Jasper, lays beige eggs with speckles. It's my Rhode Island Red, Garnet, who lays eggs the color of chocolate.

How an egg is made is fascinating and compli-cated. It takes about 26 hours to create. First the yellow germ of the yolk is released by the ovary and captured by the infundibulum, where it begins its trip down the reproductive tract. As the yolk travels, the oviduct encircles it with a fluid layer of whites, and then adds another, thicker layer of white, which includes two fibrous cords called the chalazae that hold the yolk centered in place. This jelly-like mass is then covered with two membranes, so that at this point the whole thing looks rather like a water balloon. It then moves into the uterus (also called the shell gland), where it will spend about 20 hours while the outer covering is formed.

The shell is made up almost entirely of calcium carbonate, which is a white mineral, and so all eggs start out white. The eggs that remain white have no additional pigmentation, but the potential for a wide-ranging spectrum of colors exists. The most common color is brown, with variations ranging from pale beige to a deep chocolate. The brown pigment is added during the last four to six hours of shell formation, but most of the color is added in the last 90 minutes. This is also when the cuticle, a viscous, protein-rich fluid (also called the bloom), is laid on.

As the egg moves down the passageway, it rotates. If it turns slowly, the egg will have dark speckles. A notch up in speed and there will be streaks. Sometimes, half of the egg is darker than the other, as though it had been dipped in dye. This is because the egg moves through the passage round side first. That end, pushing through, has more contact with the papillae that excrete the pigment, and thus the pigment is laid on with more pressure.

This process is even more complicated for blue egg layers. Blue pigment is a different chemical from the brown. Its scientific name is biliverdin, and it is derived from hemoglobin (a component of blood). It is metabolically costly for the hens to create. Biliverdin is added to the calcium carbonate earlier in the shell-making process, and so the eggs appear blue all the way through. Chickens that lay greenish, gray, or dusky blue eggs produce both biliverdin and brown egg pigments. The brown overlays the blue, creating a range of muted hues.

If a hen is stressed, she ceases the cuticle formation and so the shell color remains pale. Certain viral diseases and medications also decrease pigmentation. The size of the egg can affect color, too. The hen is genetically programmed to make a certain amount of pigment. If she lays a very large egg, there's less of the dye to go around. As a hen ages, she becomes less able to synthesize the colorants, and so her eggs will be lighter.

Color is not the only thing that can make an egg stand out. If you've kept chickens for any length of time, you'll probably start collecting weird eggs. I have a bowl of these misshapen, bizarrely patterned and textured eggs (blow them out and they last forever). Sometimes an eggshell's texture will be chalky, or lumpy, or look like it's covered with sand. Some eggs are wrinkled. One of my hens lays eggs that have hard shells but that look like deflated balloons. I've collected eggs that are shaped like torpedoes, and others with fat tips on both ends. Once I cracked open an egg, only to find a second shell inside! Despite how odd they look, unless they're cracked, they're all edible. (If an eggshell is cracked, bacteria is able to enter the egg, and so it's best to discard it.)

When a hen is about to lay an egg, she goes into the nesting box. Some turn around, like a dog circling before lying down. Some hens are restless layers and change position several times. Some hunker down for an hour, seemingly napping. Others get in the box and lay their eggs a few minutes later. But all hens, right before laying, stand up. Hens lay eggs standing up! The egg will be slightly damp, but it dries quickly. Some chickens squawk loudly, announcing their achievement. Others simply get up

and leave the coop. Unless a hen is broody, she has no attachment to the egg and cheerfully goes on with her day. Inside of her another yolk starts its way down her reproductive tract.

Handling and Storing Eggs (and Why the Farmstead Egg Is Safer)

In the summer of 2010, 380 million eggs were recalled due to a salmonella outbreak directly caused by the consumption of eggs from factory farms. Of course, this raised concerns about the risks of eating eggs. Rest assured that if you keep chickens in a healthy, humane environment (or buy eggs from such farms), the risk of disease is minuscule. There are reasons for this that I'll explain here. However, you still have to be careful with egg handling and storage. I'll talk about that, too.

Egg yolks are the perfect food for a developing chick inside of an egg, but they are also the perfect substrate for bacterial growth. For this reason, a hen's egg has many protective mechanisms. Obviously, the shell is the first line of defense. Thin shells crack and let in bacteria, so thick shells are best. It takes about 20 hours for a shell to become fully formed in the uterus, and the last half hour is critical. Hens tend to go into a nesting box and settle down during that time. Anxious hens that are too nervous to stay in the nesting box don't give the process enough time. Studies have shown that hens kept in cages or in crowded buildings are stressed and lay thin-shelled eggs. So it really is true that "happy hens lay healthy eggs."

Although the shell looks solid and effectively keeps large foreign particles out of the egg, it is actually covered with thousands of pores. These tiny holes let in oxygen, which is essential for a chick to grow. However, since the eggshell is permeable, it would be dangerous for the embryo to develop inside of a shell that is covered with manure and its associated pathogens. Although the egg comes out of the vent—the same orifice through which manure is passed—a section of the oviduct turns inside out as the egg is laid, which keeps the egg from touching fecal matter. It's a very clever system! The shell also has a viscous protective coating, the bloom, that prevents microbes from entering the egg.

If pathogens get past the shell, the egg has other defenses. There are two inner membranes between the shell and the white that are barriers to germs. If those membranes are breached, the egg white contains three antibacterial agents, which not only kill germs but which also inhibit the microbes' use of iron and vitamins (which they need to survive).

All of the egg's defenses are effective in normal circumstances but are strained when the egg is laid in dirt and fecal matter. When you keep your own hens, you have control over your flock's environment and can keep it clean and healthy. It's rare when I collect a dirty egg, but it happens. Once in a while a hen has a messy bottom, and so the egg is a tad dirty. Also, although hens don't defecate where and when they lay eggs, sometimes hens like to sleep in the nesting boxes, and they do poop in their sleep! I have a couple of old hens that would rather be in boxes than roost, so I clean out the pine shavings in the boxes daily using a kitty litter scoop. In the rainy springtime, my Cochin, Pearl, with her feathered feet, tracks mud onto the eggs.

If the eggs are dirty, they must be cleaned before putting them into a carton. Never store eggs with fecal matter on them—it will work its way in through those pores. Nor do you want to crack a dirty egg into a mixing bowl. Not only will your hands be contaminated, but also so will the other ingredients in your bowl. The best thing to do is to clean off the eggs when you bring them inside, before you refrigerate them. A damp paper towel is usually all that is needed to clean them up. If you have to wash the eggs, do so gently in running water that is warmer than the egg—this will cause the membrane inside of the egg to swell and prevent contaminants from entering. Don't worry about wiping off the bloom, because it's better for the egg to be clean than to keep its bloom intact. Don't go overboard in cleaning and scrub with detergents or disinfectants, as those chemicals can be pushed through the pores and you'll end up tasting and eating them. Store the eggs in clean cartons in the refrigerator, where the low temperature will further deter bacterial growth.

Storing Eggs

Many changes happen to the egg as it ages. The egg white thins and the yolks flatten. The chalazae—which look like white strings that hold the yolk centered—disappear. The fluids inside evaporate and shrink, and air pockets form. The membrane just inside the shell toughens. The egg takes on flavors and aromas from the outside, which is why it's best to keep them protected in cartons. Despite all of these changes, a refrigerated egg (at an optimal 45°F) will remain edible for 10 to 12 weeks, but will taste best within the first three.

Although fresh eggs can be left on the kitchen counter for a week or longer and still be safe to eat, it's prudent to store them in the refrigerator. Heat speeds deterioration, so during the hottest days of summer, collect the eggs from the barn at least twice a day (hens lay at any time during daylight hours) and refrigerate them immediately. Refrigeration greatly extends an egg's usefulness, as a day at a moderate room temperature equals about four days in the fridge. But a day on the counter is still better than what happens at the huge processing plants. After being washed in a hot bath, the eggs are at about 100°F when packed into the individual cartons that are eventually sold in retail markets. According to an industry trade paper, thirty dozen eggs are then packed in a case, and 30 cases are stacked onto pallets and placed into refrigerated coolers. The eggs in the middle of the pallet can take up to 142 hours—nearly six days—to cool to 45°F. The article goes on to state that a 2005 United States government report showed that if eggs were cooled and stored at 45°F within 12 hours of laying, there would be about 100,000 fewer salmonella illnesses from eggs in the nation each year. This is yet another reason why farmstead eggs from backyard hens, collected daily and put in the fridge, are a far safer food item than what comes from the industrial producers!

Long-Term Egg Storage: Freezing Eggs

Before refrigeration, people were desperate for a way to extend the shelf life of eggs. Chickens stopped laying in the winter, and the only eggs to be had were ones that had been stored. Different strategies were used: Eggs were oiled, packed in sawdust, sealed in "water-glass," pickled, and salted. I say, thank goodness for the freezer!

Egg whites can be frozen as is. It's convenient to freeze the whites in ice cube trays; one white fits into each cube pocket. Yolks, however, become gelatinous when frozen on their own, and so if freezing egg yolks, add 1 tablespoon of sugar or 1 teaspoon

of salt per 2 cups of yolks. Shelled whole eggs can be frozen, but they require ½ teaspoon of salt or 1½ tablespoons of sugar per 1 cup of eggs (about 4 large eggs). The whole eggs need to be broken up so that you no longer see the whites, but not so vigorously beaten that air is whipped in. Stirring with a fork will do. Freeze in as airtight a container as possible. Defrost in the refrigerator.

How to Tell if an Egg Is Fresh

When you collect eggs from your own hens, you know exactly how fresh they are. Usually. Sometimes, though, the hen decides to lay somewhere other than the nesting box and you find a clutch of eggs under a rosebush or behind a wheelbarrow. Sometimes a hen lays an egg in the nesting box but you don't know how old it is because it's been hidden under the shavings. Sometimes there's a heat spell and the coop has been more than 100°F and you worry that the eggs may not be all right. (High temperatures cause rapid deterioration of eggs.) Once in a while you might buy eggs and not be sure how old they are. For all of these reasons, it's good to have a simple method to test whole eggs for freshness.

First, though, it helps to understand what happens to an egg as it ages. The shell, although it looks solid, is covered with between 7,000 and 12,000 tiny pores. The pores are potential entry points for bacteria and aromas. Despite this, eggs in optimal conditions—clean, collected soon after laying, chilled promptly, and kept at 45°F—remain edible for 12 weeks. Conditions, of course, aren't always optimal.

As the egg ages, it loses carbon dioxide and moisture through the pores. This changes the pH inside the egg and makes it more basic, which in turn affects the egg whites. Over time, the whites go from cloudy to clear and from thick to thin. The yolk flattens. The chalazae, those protein strings that hold the yolk in the center, disintegrate. The membranes surrounding the whites separate. An air pocket forms. It's that air pocket that gives us the ability to test for freshness.

Fill a bowl with water and set the egg in the bottom. A just-laid egg will lie there horizontally. I use these freshest of eggs for frying and poaching. An egg about a week old will tip ever so slightly up. They're also fine for frying, and for all other uses except hard-cooking. By two weeks, the egg's pointy end will lift off of the bottom of the bowl. These are the eggs that I use for hard-cooking, as they are still delicious but are now easily peeled. When the eggs stand upright in the bowl, they are near their expiration date. I'll use those in cakes, but not in recipes that require whipped whites. If an egg floats, it is no longer edible and should be thrown out. When it is this old, the outside looks the same, but inside the egg has gone through changes in pH, flavor, and texture. It has been around long enough that it could be riddled with unseen bacteria. If cracked open, it will spread out so thin as to be unusable, and it might smell very, very bad. It's best to trust the float test and not open it to see!

A Note on Egg Safety

All foods carry some risk of going bad or harboring disease. Eggs are no exception. Farmstead eggs have many defenses against carrying infectious agents (see page 22), but there is always a very slight chance of contracting salmonella or another bacterial disease from undercooked eggs. I have full confidence in the eggs from my hens and eat

them soft-cooked and raw in meringues, and I treat myself to the uncooked cookie batter out of bowls. What I don't do is leave eggs out unrefrigerated, and I am careful to keep preparations with raw eggs, such as homemade mayonnaise, chilled. If you are pregnant or have a compromised immune system, you might want to stick to recipes that specify fully cooked eggs.

The Risk of Chicken-to-Human Disease Transmission

All animals, from crustaceans to humans, are hosts, both inside and out, to multitudes of bacteria. Many of these microbes perform essential functions, from aiding digestion to making nutrients available for use. But there are also germs that cause disease, like *E. coli*. They're ever present, but they are kept in check in a healthy system.

Farmstead chickens carry around their share of germs, and it's prudent to worry about whether we can get sick from them. The quick answer is that there are very few diseases that humans and birds share. Our biologies are just too different. That said, there are a small number of pathogens to know about, all of which can be neutralized by good hand-washing practices and conscientious animal husbandry. The truly scary diseases are not coming from backyard flocks; they originate in animal factories (let's not call them "farms"). I'm not going to go into a diatribe about how factory production facilities that rely on antibiotics to keep their animals alive are creating "superbugs" that are resistant to drugs, or how these places are so overcrowded with feces, dust, and vermin that the pathogen load is overwhelming. I'm sure you've read this ongoing story in the press. Instead, let's go over what you need to know about the hens in your backyard.

The biggest fear that many have is of bird flu. My readers in North America don't have to worry about this. We've never had a case here of avian influenza of the type that affects human health. For people in other parts of the world, it appears that actually coming down with the disease requires close contact with the dead bird (such as when people strip the feathers off deceased swans). In Asia, avian influenza shows up in people who are living in close contact with large numbers of birds, and it's usually waterfowl, not chickens.

Another disease that you might have heard is zoonotic (transmissible from animal to human) is Newcastle disease. Rest assured that it isn't of great concern for backyard poultry keepers. In chickens it causes respiratory ailments. Transmitted to humans, it triggers mild conjunctivitis, but even this is usually only seen in people who administer the Newcastle vaccine to poultry, or lab workers who do necropsies. Two other zoonotic diseases are erysipelas and chlamydiosis, which are mostly hosted by turkeys and affect only humans who work in slaughterhouses and farmers of large flocks. Avian tuberculosis is another one that is quite rare (it's more prevalent with parrot fanciers) but possible to contract. Internal and external parasites are species specific and, as nasty as lice and worms look, they're not going to infect your gut if you somehow ingest them.

The three bacterial pathogens that are of concern are *Salmonella spp.*, *Campylobacter spp.*, and *E. coli.* Generally people get sickened by these bugs after eating improperly cooked and handled meat and eggs that have been contaminated with the germs, not by handling live and healthy chickens. Yes, poultry harbor these pathogens in their systems, but simply washing your hands with soap and hot water after holding your hens is generally enough to prevent disease transmission. One exception that occurred recently involved chicks from large hatcheries. Children who kissed the chicks came down with salmonella. This is a serious enough concern that the CDC (Center for Disease Control and Prevention) issued a statement advising people not to snuggle with or kiss their chicks, which is advice that certainly makes sense. Besides, I don't think that chicks like being kissed, and it's not necessary for socializing them. Gently holding chicks in your hands, then washing up afterward, is best for both you and the fluffy babies.

Other issues that might come up (but that aren't transmissible diseases) are allergies, as well as respiratory irritations due to mold and dust. Some people are allergic to the dander that chickens are constantly generating as they grow and shed feathers. Chickens also create a fine dust out of bedding material and manure that they shred to bits as they scratch the ground. Sometimes bedding or feed will become moldy, especially if there's been a long rainy period. Any respiratory and allergic reactions to these irritants can be minimized by housing the chickens in a well-ventilated and dry coop and by practicing good manure management.

An article published by the Penn State College of Agricultural Sciences put it like this: "People should not fear close association with poultry as a significant human health risk." So enjoy your hens. Handle them and spend time with them. Just don't kiss them.

Choosing Chickens

You've decided that you want to raise chickens and cultivate your own eggs. Before you spend any money, consider this list of reasons to own—or not own—chickens.

The Pros and Cons of Keeping Backyard Hens

Sometimes, it's all in how you look at it.

PROS	CONS
Fresh eggs	Seasonal supply; sometimes no eggs
Beautiful eggs of many hues, shapes, and sizes	Weird-looking eggs; some too small for recipes, some too big
Knowing exactly what goes into the eggs because you've supplied their feed	Spending a lot of money on feed and having to make trips to the feed store
Chickens eat kitchen leftovers	Having to save and handle kitchen refuse
A daily supply of manure to be composted for the garden	Manure (and flies and smell)
The pleasure of chatty, cheerful hens	Noisy, demanding hens
A coop that adds to the garden décor	A building that takes up too much space
The hens scratch up bugs in the garden	The hens make dust wallows in the garden
Daily chores to get you outside	Daily chores in the dark, rain, and cold
Old hens that become pets	Old hens that are useless
An appreciation for the cycle of life and knowledge that death is part of that	Chickens get sick and die, which is depressing
There's no pro to having an unexpected rooster in the flock	What was supposed to be a hen is a rooster and no one wants him

Still determined to raise chickens? Here's how to get started.

How Many Hens to Keep?

There's no perfect answer to the question, "How many hens should I keep?" Chickens don't lay the same number of eggs day in and day out, year in and year out. Depending on the breed and the individual hen, at the peak of production you'll get three to six eggs per week. But hens go broody, they molt, and heat and cold stress them. During the shorter daylight hours of winter, their laying frequency wanes. As they age they lay fewer and fewer eggs until they stop laying altogether. If you want a sure supply of eggs all year long, you'll either need a large flock or be willing to cull your old hens and start fresh every two years. I have the room, and so I keep the retired hens, and every few years I bring in chicks to replenish the layers. Even with this flexibility, I go through stretches of not having enough eggs for the kitchen. That said, a half a dozen chickens is plenty if you're looking for enough fresh eggs with which to make breakfast a few mornings a week and an occasional bounty to splurge with.

Chickens are social animals and need to live with others of their kind. Even if you have a small space, don't keep only one. Three is a good start for social interactions; seven is better. That's because chickens are quite particular as to whom they chose to hang out with. Just because you put two hens together to keep each other company doesn't mean that they'll like each other. With three hens, even if they're not best buddies, the dynamics will be more sociable. With more hens, you'll have a few solid friendships and the other hens will be content to hang out on the fringes. Don't worry that you'll have too many eggs. Friends and neighbors are always willing to take the overflow.

Choosing the Right Chicken Breed for You

The domestic chicken is the descendant of the jungle fowl of Asia. Like all animals that have followed an evolutionary path with humans, chickens have changed in utility and appearance. To earn their keep in the farmyard, chickens had to produce more eggs and carry more meat on their frame than jungle fowl do in the wild. But that doesn't explain why there is a dizzying array of chicken breeds. The American Poultry Association, which is the arbiter of the "Standard of Perfection" (as described in a book of the same name), recognizes more than 60 breeds, with variations within each. Few of the traits of these domesticated birds are linked to egg and meat production; most have come about because people care

what chickens look like. Even people with hobby farms, who expect their hens to produce enough to repay their investment, find themselves making decisions based on looks. Go to a poultry exhibition (similar to a dog show, at which chickens are judged on their appearance and how true to type they are) and you'll see poultry garbed in a vast array of feathers: some that look like fur, others that are twisted and curled, and some feathers that are several times longer than the chicken itself. You'll see chickens in colors from white to golden to black (with many in between) and in patterns from polka-dotted to striped. Some chickens have poufy topknots on their heads, and others have no feathers on their necks at all. There are chickens with tall combs, long combs that flop over, and stubby combs. Legs come in a range of colors, too, from yellow to red to gray. Egg color varies as well, in hues from white to brown to blue to green.

Before deciding on the breeds you want, decide on the number of chickens and stick to it! Three is the minimum, as I've just mentioned, but better yet is to have five hens. That will assure you of an egg or more a day and better flock dynamics. More than five hens requires a commitment in housing and space that you might not want to make until you've had a flock for a while. Chicken hatcheries send out catalogs in the winter when we're wistfully thinking about all of the eggs that will be laid again come spring. Some of us look at hatchery catalogs like the proverbial child in a candy shop. The illustrations of the different poultry breeds look so appealing that we want one of each. I heard about a man who tried to collect a hen of every type, but he stopped at 89. Don't be swayed by the photographs into ordering more than you can keep. Overcrowding causes health and behavior issues (see page 35 for more about space requirements for your flock).

Just like a dog lover doesn't necessarily love all breeds equally, a chicken fancier finds some chickens more to his or her liking than others. Of all the chicken breeds, I have a few favorites, but my choices might not be best for you. Just like some people prefer border collies and others like pugs, some people like Polish chickens and others Buff Orpingtons. That said, there are some practical criteria to use when deciding which breeds of chickens to get.

The first option is whether to get standard-size chickens, which are the large ones (4 to 6 pounds), or bantams, which are smaller (less than 2 pounds). Bantams do have some advantages. They can be housed in smaller coops, and they tend not to damage the garden as much with their foraging. I think that a bantam White Leghorn is the perfect hen to introduce poultry to young children. Leghorns are friendly, active, and quiet. Other small chickens are also wonderful for children. Silkies, in particular, are placid and sweet (although they do need extra care in the winter). However, if having a full egg basket is your goal, then bantams are not the best choice, as they tend to go broody (and thus stop laying) and when they do lay, their eggs are quite small.

If egg production is the most important criteria on your list of traits, then choose a hybrid. Each hatchery has its own cross, which is usually between a Leghorn and a brown-egg layer. They're nice, solid, friendly birds. They're good foragers, calm, pleasant, rarely broody, and excellent layers. Another hybrid is the sex-link, so called because the male and female chicks are feathered differently. If you order sex-links, you don't have to worry that a chick will grow up to be a rooster.

Also take into account the weather in your area. In New England, where I live, it's prudent to get hens that are winter hardy. These tend to have smaller combs and are well feathered to provide protection from the cold. I like clean-legged breeds because the ones with feathers down to their toes get muddy and icy, while the ones with bare legs stay clean and dry.

Some hens don't do well in hot climes. Cochins and other "soft-feathered" varieties have more and fluffier feathers than other breeds. They overheat easily. I have only one Cochin, named Pearl, who pants and hides in the shade as soon as the weather warms up in the summer. She requires extra care, but Pearl is worth it because she has the typical sweet and gentle Cochin personality. On the other end of the spectrum is the sleek White Leghorn, which is well adapted for hot weather. Leghorns have fewer insulating down feathers and their big combs help to dissipate body heat. Leghorns are friendly and active hens and do fine in New England, but in areas with more severe winter weather their combs are prone to frostbite.

Some people make a decision about chicken breed based solely on the color of the eggs. A singular pleasure of having backyard hens is collecting a basket of eggs of many hues. Araucana hens lay bright blue eggs, Marans lay chocolate brown eggs, Leghorns lay alabaster white eggs, and other hens lay speckled, beige, and even green eggs. Choosing hens based on egg color is a valid way to select the birds for your flock.

Once you get chickens, you'll notice differences in personality between the breeds, and you will likely develop strong preferences. I've heard, "I don't like Ameraucanas, they're too aloof," and "I love my Orpingtons, such gentle birds!" Talk to me and you're going to hear tales about my Speckled Sussex hens, who are all curious and rather dotty individuals. But just because I love them, it doesn't mean that they're for everyone. Speckled Sussex hens are not calm and docile!

I like to keep a flock with a mix of breeds. I like being able to identify hens from a distance by sight, and I like the mix of personalities and the range of colors in my egg basket. Although it is generally true that hens congregate with others that look like them, you can have a peaceful and happy flock composed of a number of breeds. You can even mix bantams and standard hens if you have enough space. However, I've found that some breeds don't do well confined in pens with more docile hens. For example, Barred Plymouth Rocks, Rhode Island Reds, and Wyandottes are all great foragers and need an environment in which they can be actively eating and exploring all day. Kept in a small coop with meeker birds like Welsummers, they can turn into bullies. Also, Polish hens, with their crazily feathered heads and ditzy personalities, can be the targets of aggression. Extra space and outside roosts help to alleviate these sorts of problems.

So, there is no definitive answer as to which breeds are best for starting your farmstead flock. All of the online hatcheries have detailed descriptions of each breed's egg production and other traits, and these are worth perusing. Get a variety and soon enough you'll form your own conclusions about the perfect breeds. In my own experience, that list has changed as I've added different hens into the mix.

Chicken Keeping

I'm delighted that more and more people are collecting eggs from their own backyard flocks. However, chicken keeping isn't for everyone. Putting a few chickens in a coop in the backyard takes as much thought and responsibility as bringing home a puppy. A backyard flock isn't cheap, and it's not glamorous. But for me, the benefits outweigh the time, expense, and trouble. What follows is what you need to know to decide whether you, too, should have a chicken-keeping life.

An Introduction to Chicken Keeping

Hens are bossy, demanding, endlessly curious, and easily gratified. They are comical to watch, make great friends to your children, provide amusement for you, and supply eggs for the table. I've enjoyed keeping chickens for almost 20 years. Currently, I have 17 hens. Twelve are young and in the prime of their egg-laying years. Five are old and retired. I'm not a real farmer and can afford to keep hens that do not lay daily, and so my chickens are dual-purpose—egg layers and pets.

What I don't have is a rooster. Hens lay eggs whether a rooster is around or not. This is a good thing, as many communities have zoning regulations that allow hen keeping but prohibit roosters. My town has no such restrictions, but I don't want the boys. Roosters crow all day, not just in the morning. Many roosters are aggressive and will attack anyone coming into their space. Also, they constantly try to mate with the hens. My girls appear quite content to not have a male in their midst. Although I've been told that a rooster will keep the peace in the flock, my hens have no problems settling mild squabbles on their own. Some people, though, do like having a rooster around, what with his big personality and voice and watchfulness for predators. It is possible to find a nice (though not quiet) rooster, so never settle for one that attacks people!

You'll need to provide your chickens with a henhouse to give them shelter from inclement weather, a place to lay eggs, and a safe haven to spend the night. It doesn't have to be elaborate or huge, although a fanciful coop can be a feature of your garden design. The more space your chickens have, the healthier and happier they'll be. (Learn more about coops on page 35.) The term "pecking order" definitely originated with poultry. Chickens peck at each other for all sorts of reasons, but mostly to keep the other girls away from their treasures, be it a glistening drop of rain or a juicy bug. Given enough space, these little spats are harmless, but when chickens are crowded, they become ruthless bullies. (There's more about pecking order on page 43.) Housed properly and given plenty to do, your hens will be charming and friendly to you and each other.

During the day, chickens need access to sunshine and an outdoor run. They need places to scratch and things to do. One of the great pleasures of chicken keeping is watching your flock coming and going. It's a bit of a paradox—hens are always busy, and yet watching them is calming. I compare it to going to the ocean. The waves are in constant motion, and yet the overall experience is peaceful.

Chickens need a dry and loose patch of earth to dust-bathe in, which is one of their favorite things to do. They'll lie down and kick dirt under their feathers.

They'll preen and nap in the sun. Sometimes several hens at a time will dust-bathe together in a sociable group. Not only is this an enjoyable activity for the hens, but it also keeps them healthy by killing off external parasites. I put a kitty litter box filled with coarse sand in the coop so that the hens have a place to dirt-bathe year-round, even when there is snow on the ground.

Hens need access to chicken feed and water all day long. Although the commercial ration should make up the bulk of your flock's diet, chickens are omnivores and eat a wide range of foodstuffs. One of the benefits of having a backyard flock is that kitchen scraps that would otherwise be thrown out get consumed with such gusto! All of this eating does mean that there is quite a bit of manure produced. I am obsessive about keeping the coops clean and the manure composted. Not only does this control parasites, flies, and odor, but properly made compost becomes the best garden dirt ever.

The first two years are the hen's most productive. After that egg laying declines, and by the age of five a chicken lays as few as an egg or two a week. Although chickens are not long-lived, most will live past the age of two, and so the problem arises of what to do with older hens. People who keep chickens solely for the food that they provide harvest (that is, eat) their laying hens when they reach 18 months of age. But most of us with backyard chickens don't do that. The older hens in my flock become familiar faces in my backyard, and I enjoy having them around even though they rarely lay. Every few years I add new hens to the group in order to have a supply of eggs for my table. If you live in a town that limits the number of chickens allowed in a flock, this might not be possible, and at some point you will have hens but not be getting any eggs at all. So, as you begin your chicken-keeping life, think through these issues. I can tell you that once you get a few hens, you'll likely want more. Have fun!

A Hen's Life Cycle

Most backyard chickens are purchased as chicks from large hatcheries. The three-day-old chicks arrive at the post office inside a cardboard box. A chick can survive just fine for a couple of days after hatching without any food and water because it gets nourishment from the yolk that is inside its body. But by the time your small flock arrives at your house, the chicks will need water, food, and a comfortable place to grow.

The first month or two (depending on the weather) is spent in a brooder, which is a secure home that is warmed with a heat lamp. The chicks need special care during those first weeks. Online hatcheries have very good advice on how to care for them, so I will not go into it here. The chicks are adorable—so fluffy! But within a week they start to shed their down. Feathers grow in, which appear first as spiny quills, making the chicks look like baby pterodactyls. You'll be tempted to keep the chicks in a box in the kitchen. Don't. The dander from the feather-growing process coats everything with a fine and sticky dust. Chicks also scratch the ground just like adult chickens do. They'll shred their bedding and their poop into tiny particles that mingle with the dander dust in the air. It's much better to have a brooder out in the garage, or better yet, the coop.

The chicks grow quickly and will need an increasingly larger space. By eight weeks the chicks will be tall and gawky. If the weather is warm they'll be able to go outside and move from the brooder into the coop. By three months you'll be looking at the chickens and wondering if one or more of them is a rooster. One might be larger, louder, bossier. Sometimes you can tell early on, but sometimes you don't know for sure until you hear one of them crowing.

By four months they'll look full-grown and you'll be ready to start collecting eggs, but you'll need a bit of patience yet. At this point, and until they reach the age of one year, the young female hens are called pullets. Some pullets lay by 17 weeks, but others don't produce their first eggs until they are six months old. Partly this variation is due to genetics, as some breeds are slower to mature. When your pullets start laying is also affected by the weather and time of year. Extreme heat and, conversely, chilly temps inhibit laying. If your young birds reach maturity during the shorter, darker days of winter, they won't begin to lay until springtime. Stress can affect when they lay, too. For example, a lurking predator, moving the pullets into new quarters, or suddenly bringing a dog into your life (that harasses the birds) can all set the laying schedule back. However, if all goes well, by the time your chickens are 18 weeks old, you'll start collecting the first eggs.

Depending on the individual hen and her breed, she'll lay anywhere from three to five eggs a week. If the chicks were hatched in the early springtime, then you'll see the first eggs in late summer. Depending on many factors (including sunlight, temperature, and the individual hen), you might get eggs through that first winter. By the time she is one year old she'll be laying at full tilt. That is, unless she goes broody. A broody hen sits in a nesting box for weeks without laying. She thinks she is going to hatch eggs. She'll do this even if there are no eggs under her. She'll huff up in anger at any interruption of her focus on the setting of her (imaginary) eggs. She'll leave the nesting box only once a day to eat, drink, and leave a foul "broody poop." This is especially frustrating for the urban chicken keeper who has only three hens, as the broody one stops laying, takes up space in the nesting box, and is an unpleasant creature to be around. Some breeds of chickens are prone to broodiness (for example, Silkies and Buff Orpingtons), while others almost never go broody (like Leghorns and Golden Comets). It is possible to break the broody spell, but it takes four days of separation from the flock in a wire-floored hutch to bring down her body temperature and stop the raging hormones.

Before factory farms (where chickens are housed indoors in artificial environments), eggs were seasonal (chickens need 14 hours of daylight to lay daily), and winter eggs were rare and expensive. In a farmstead flock, winter continues to be the downtime. Your pullets start laying in the fall of their first year, and might, depending on breed and conditions, lay sporadically through that first winter. The next summer, when they are a year old, is the prime laying time. Then, when a chicken is 16 to 18 months of age, she molts. She loses her feathers and needs to put all of her resources into growing a new coat. Laying stops for anywhere from six to ten weeks. Because this happens at the start of the winter, I do not leave a light on to encourage egg laying. I feel that my hens need and deserve a break. Because the hens don't all molt at the same time, and because I have a dozen laying hens, I'm never entirely without eggs during the winter, although there are weeks when I collect only three or four. I adjust my menus accordingly. I no longer have two eggs every morning for breakfast and I don't make puddings. Fortunately, I live near a small family farm that does keep chickens that lay all winter. (This farm keeps pullets inside with electric bulbs.) I purchase their eggs when I run out of my own stash and can't do without. By February the best layers resume egg production, and as spring turns into summer they all do. However, in their second year most hens lay 20 percent fewer eggs than their first year, and some will lay far less than that. Hens lay through that second summer, until once again they molt as winter is coming on. The molt happens every year, and every year production decreases and the time it takes to complete molting increases. As the hens get older, other changes happen, too: Eggshells thin and crack, and egg quality decreases. Health issues and deaths in the aging flock increase.

As much as many of us love our chickens solely for their charm and character, it's important to understand that their primary reason for being has historically been for use as farm animals. Because laying hens are most productive in their first two years, they've never been bred to last longer. I have poultry books from a hundred years ago that recommend culling the poor layers (and putting them into the stew pot) after the first molt and all others by the second. (Past that age a chicken is not worth eating.) From a farmer's perspective, this makes sense. What this means for those of us who have laying hens that become pets is that we have to deal with many issues that professional farmers, even those who kept small homesteads in the 1800s, have never had to face.

The best layers are usually the first to die, probably because after a couple of years of producing eggs, they are worn out. Some die suddenly, and some look poorly for weeks on end. Other hens keep going. They lay fewer and fewer eggs, but they live, year after year. Their molts take longer, they

forage less, and they nap more. The majority of hens don't make it past five, but a few will keep on, even producing an egg now and then. There are many ailments that can cause death. Chickens are prone to cancer. They have a multitude of reproductive tract diseases. Respiratory infections can sweep through a flock. Despite this, it is rare, but it happens, that a hen will live for a dozen years.

It's crucial that a person who is thinking about keeping a few chickens in the backyard takes into account that a hen can live long after she is no longer productive. If there are zoning restrictions on flock size, what will you do when all of your hens are too old to lay? Some people choose to cull at two years, when feeding the chicken costs more than the value of the eggs that she lays. Others will keep the old hens on as pets. If that's your decision, then it's also important to understand that hens get sick, that veterinary help is hard to find, and when it is available, it's often prohibitively expensive and rarely effective. Anyone who keeps chickens will face making very difficult end-of-life decisions.

For me, despite the ailments and lack of eggs, by the time a hen stops laying, she's become part of the fabric of my backyard community. There's something deeply satisfying about getting to know an animal over the years. I don't depend on farming for my livelihood, and I can afford to keep elderly chickens around. I'm committed to giving the older hens a good quality of life until the end. I have an extensive collection of poultry books, both vintage and current, but care of old hens is still new territory. I've learned much from my own chickens; it's an ongoing education, and what I find out I share on my website in FAQs and blog posts.

ELEMENTS OF LIFE CYCLE	
1 to 3 days	chick lives off yolk
hatching to 8 weeks	chicks live in heated brooder
8 weeks to "point of lay" (17 to 22 weeks)	chicks mature
17 weeks to 16 months	most productive laying stage
around 16 months	first molt lasts 6 to 10 weeks
2 to 2½ years (early spring until late fall)	second laying season
2½ years	second molt
3 to 3½ years (early spring until late fall)	third laying season (production declines; chicken is considered old)

What Do a Dozen Backyard Eggs Cost?

There are many reasons to keep backyard hens, but not one of them is to have a cheap source of eggs. Supermarket eggs are very inexpensive and despite their shortcomings are a superior source of nutrition, especially for someone on a limited budget. There's no way that I can raise eggs at that price point.

Let's ignore, for now, the initial cost of setup—the housing, fencing, feeder, and waterer. Ignore, too, the cost of the chicks and the weeks of feeding them before they lay. Ignore the old and retired hens that you keep around because they've become pets. Let's just look at the cost of caring for a productive backyard laying hen.

A hen is a voracious eater. She needs to eat a lot because making eggs is depleting. What goes in comes right back out. Each day she expels 2 to 3 ounces of manure, plus an egg that weighs 2 ounces and is mostly protein covered in calcium. It's important that she's fed well because those outputs strain her system. Although a chicken is an omnivore and can seemingly happily fill up on kitchen scraps like stale bread and garden weeds, she won't stay healthy or lay sturdy eggs unless she gets a balanced diet. The way to ensure that is to feed her laying hen pellets, sold in 50-pound bags at the feed store. "It's just chicken feed" is an expression that means that something isn't worth much. You can no longer say it about chicken feed! The cost of grain has risen and continues to rise. A 50-pound bag of laying hen feed costs anywhere from $16 to $20, and much more if you buy organic. If your hen doesn't get anything other than the pellets, she'll eat at least ¼ pound or more a day. Hens that have access to a compost bin with kitchen scraps (and worms!) or that free-range will eat fewer pellets, but figure that it costs about 10¢ a day for just the feed. You'll also need oyster shell, and you'll probably offer treats like sunflower seeds and cracked corn. Factor in bags of shavings ($7 each) for bedding. Just to throw out a number, as all backyard setups are different, let's say it costs 15¢ a day to feed and bed your hen. That's only $54 a year.

But no hen lays every day: She'll stop during the winter and she'll stop during a molt. She might also stop laying if it is very hot, or dark and rainy. If she's broody, she'll stop laying then, too. The very best layer might provide 280 eggs per year, but some hens don't lay at all and others leave just 100 eggs in the nesting boxes over the course of the year. Let's say you have one hen that during her best laying year gave you 200 eggs. Each of those eggs cost 27¢, or $3.24 a dozen, which is about what you'd pay at the market for good eggs, although not as much as organic. But since fresh eggs from your own hens are not something that you can buy elsewhere, it's like the tagline for the credit card ad: priceless.

The reality in my own flock is nowhere near that

$3 a dozen. Of the 17 hens currently residing in my backyard, five are retired and don't lay at all. Of the young and productive year-old hens, two are Buff Orpingtons that spent the prime laying days of the summer being broody. A couple are pretty hens that lay only three eggs a week. They all take a break from laying in the winter. One year I kept an exact accounting of how much it cost to care for my flock and exactly how many eggs they laid. Let's just say that the eggs didn't cost more than what I'd pay for the most expensive organic eggs at the pricey market. I haven't kept records since.

Coop Design

Coops can be elaborate or rustic. They can cost a lot of money or be made out of discarded wood pallets. Because the coops in my backyard are part of my landscaped garden, I like them to be beautiful. But none of that matters to the hens. Your chickens will be happy and healthy as long as their housing meets their basic needs.

Giving your hens enough space is critical to their well-being. Crowded chickens become aggressive and might peck until there is bloodshed or, in the worst scenario, death. At the minimum each hen needs 4 square feet of floor space inside the coop. This does not include the roosts or the nesting boxes or the outside pen. Be wary of prefab coops for sale that state they are appropriate for "up to 12 hens." Do not believe it; do the math yourself. Outside, each hen requires an additional 8 square feet (at least!).

Inside the coop there should be roosting bars for the chickens to sleep on. I've found that 1- to 1½-inch rounded dowels are satisfactory for both my bantams and my standard-size hens. My first coop had a branch cut from a tree. It provided

COST OF SETTING UP A SMALL BACKYARD FLOCK

This chart gives a general idea of the costs involved, but prices vary depending on the manufacturer.	
Coop The handy can make it out of recycled materials, others can buy prefab structures.	$100–$2,000
Fencing All pens need to be kept secure with wire fencing installed 6 inches underground. Chicken wire costs $150 per 100-foot roll (6 feet high). Stakes are $10 each.	$150–$1,000
Hawk netting to protect the run from aerial predators	$60
Feeder	$25
Water fount	$25
Water fount heater base (for cold climates)	$60
Oyster shell dispenser	$15
Galvanized cans to store feed	$25
Cleaning tools	$25
Pullets at point of lay	$25 each
Muck bucket	$20
Pitchfork	$25
Rake	$20
Plastic scrub brush to clean waterer	$4

OTHER, NOT SO ESSENTIAL, ITEMS

Treats, such as hulled sunflower seeds and cabbages
Suet holder to hold treats
Kitty litter box for dust baths
Coarse sand for dust baths
Egg basket (much better than pockets!)* (*Everyone I know has collected an egg, slipped it into a jacket pocket, and forgotten it! Besides, having hens is a great excuse to buy a beautiful wire basket, preferably antique.)
Egg scale

various-size perches for my different-size hens. Each chicken needs 6 inches of space on the roosts. I like to offer them bars at several heights, like a ladder leaning against the wall. (Actually, a real wooden ladder makes a great roost. I use one in my barn.) My heavier and older hens need lower roosts so that they can get up and down.

Chickens lay eggs in nesting boxes. They're exactly like cubbyholes; a 12-inch square is a good size, but hens are flexible. What the hen does care about is that the boxes are not in bright sunlight and that they feel safe and cozy. Installing nesting boxes lower than the roosts discourages the hens from sleeping in them. If you have fewer than five hens, have two nesting boxes. For larger flocks, have one box for every five hens. Also, there should be room inside the coop, or under dry cover, for food and water dispensers.

The coop should have windows. Chickens have terrible night vision, and if the coop is dark they can't see their way inside or out in the morning and will miss out on valuable eating time. Most important, if chickens are housed in the dark they will lay fewer eggs.

The coop needs to be well ventilated but not drafty. Not only do chickens need floor space, but they also require air space. I'm seeing too many coops that are no larger than doghouses; there's barely room for the hens to stand and the "roosts" are on the floor. Chicken manure is 75 percent water, and a large component is nitrogen. As this decomposes, ammonia fumes are created. Small coops, especially those without windows or those with windows that are shuttered closed during inclement weather, don't allow for an exchange of fresh air. Large vents in the eaves help. A functioning cupola is an excellent addition to all designs.

The hens enter and exit the coop through a "pop-door," which is an opening about a foot square and a foot from the floor. Unless there's a raging storm outside, I keep this door open all day. It lets in fresh air, and the hens like to see what's going on outside. At night I latch it closed to keep out predators.

There are other things to consider when building a coop. Chicken feed comes in 50-pound sacks. Pine shavings for bedding are sold in large rectangular bags. You'll need a muck bucket, a pitchfork, and a rake for cleaning out the coop. Waterers need scrubbing with a brush reserved for that task. It's convenient to have a storage area for all of these things in part of the coop or in a shed right next door.

One other thing to think through is how the coop restricts or encourages your interactions with the flock. If the coop is small and closed up, then you can't see what they're doing inside. If fencing over the outdoor run is too low to allow you to enter, you can't keep the pen clean and you can't visit with your chickens. Children, especially, like to go into a coop and sit companionably with the hens. My preference is for both the coop and run to be tall and spacious enough to accommodate a human guest. I like watching the hens go in and out of the nesting boxes. I like watching the nighttime roosting ritual and hearing the bedtime clucking lullaby. This is why I have coops that I can walk into. An added benefit is that larger coops have better air quality and so your hens will be healthier. However, a coop doesn't have to be huge. My first henhouse was a 4- by 6-foot prefab garden shed that we converted into a coop. It was big enough for five hens and storage. It was also large enough for my son, then in kindergarten, to carry a stool inside and visit with his chicken friends.

Daily and Weekly Chores

Caring for a small flock of backyard hens does not take a lot of time. The daily chores can be done in minutes in the morning and a few more in the evening. Chickens sleep inside a coop at night. I keep mine latched into secure housing, as the danger of predators grabbing a chicken dinner in the dark is ever-present. First thing in the morning, I go out to the coop and open the pop-door. After many years of doing this daily I still get pleasure from watching them hustle out, eager to see what the day has in store for them. Chickens are optimistic animals, and I can't help but have some of their morning joy rub off on me. If you cannot be there soon after sunrise, you can install an automatic door opener (there are several on the market designed specifically for coops).

After the hens are let out, I check that they have feed and water. Pellets are dispensed from a galvanized tin hopper that holds 10 pounds and so requires refilling only once a week. Water comes out of a fount that needs filling only once every few days. But I'm not complacent about checking the food and water daily, as I never know what mischief the chickens will get into. The feed and water dispensers could be dirty, tipped over, or broken. I also do a quick check to see if there is manure in the nesting boxes. If there is, I take a kitty litter scoop and clean it out. Taking one minute to do this saves having to clean eggs later. That's it for the morning chores. The girls can be left to their own devices until evening. At some point during the day, I take a basket out to the coop and check for eggs, which is always an enjoyable task.

Chickens put themselves to bed at night. Come sundown they'll mosey into the coop and clamber onto the roosts to sleep. Every night I close the door behind them to keep out predators. This might be my favorite moment of the day with the hens, as they murmur a contented lullaby of low clucks and chortles as they settle in.

Keeping the coop and run clean and removing manure is a chore I perform once or twice a week. I use pine shavings inside the henhouse. This bedding is absorbent and smells good. A fine-tined pitchfork (a plastic tool available at most feed stores) makes quick work of picking up the manure and leaving the good shavings behind. Since chickens eventually scratch even the clean shavings into a fine dust, every few months I take a shovel and remove everything and start fresh. Once a week I take a flexible metal rake to the hard-packed dirt in their pen to remove manure. The manure goes into a compost bin out by the garden. In half a year it becomes rich, fertile soil.

There is one more thing that I do daily, and that is to take a moment to be with the hens. It's a companionable time. I watch each chicken, taking note of her demeanor and behavior. Chickens will hide illness until they are very sick. Sometimes an ailment can come on suddenly and kill in a day. Often the first sign that something is amiss is a change in social behavior or a slight drop in appetite. I know each individual and so I am able to spot early on when something is wrong. Paying attention is probably the most important daily chore there is. Even more than collecting the eggs, knowing the hens and having a relationship with them is what makes the work worthwhile.

How Noisy Are Hens?

We all know that roosters are loud, what with their cock-a-doodle-doing all day long. That's one reason why towns and cities ban the boys. Always check with your town hall before getting your flock. The board of health or the zoning board will fill you in on your community's regulations. It's true that hens don't crow, but that doesn't mean that your flock will be quietly unobtrusive. Sure, some hens go about their days saying nothing. Others chuck-chuck and bawk-bawk in low pitches, almost under their breath, like they're talking to themselves. Some only up the volume when they've laid their eggs, announcing the achievement with a quick squawk and then returning to their quiet lives.

But other hens are loud. Very loud. Onyx, my Barnevelder, is a talker. She broadcasts that she's stepped into the coop. She lets everyone know that she's going back outside. A half an hour before laying an egg, she'll increase the volume while stomping around the barn. Etheldred, a Speckled Sussex, is another one that wants to be heard, and her clucking isn't pretty. Her tone of voice is that of someone complaining loudly at a service desk in a department store.

But neither of these two girls compares to my late New Hampshire Red hen, Marge. She and her twin sister, Petunia, always traveled side by side, but it was easy to tell them apart. You knew Marge by her vocalizations. She was like an ever-present haranguing, argumentative, and demanding aunt. She'd watch me garden, constantly clucking in what sounded like a stream of criticisms. "You're doing what?" "Not there!" "Toss me the bug, now!" Petunia never said a word. Marge had such an insistent, unique voice that I made it into a ringtone. I have

it on my iPhone clock. When I put money into a parking meter, I set the timer to remind me when the time is up. There's nothing like having Marge squawking at me to get me running to the car.

Most hens aren't disturbingly vocal like Marge and Onyx. The low, happy chortle of busy and happy chickens is one of the pleasures of keeping a backyard flock. The problem is, you will have no idea whether you have obnoxiously noisy hens until they are full-grown and laying. Some breeds are known to be more talkative than others. Speckled Sussex and Rhode Island Reds do cluck. Others, like the Buff Orpingtons and the Leghorns, are quieter. But there are always exceptions that don't follow breed guidelines.

When you have a loud hen (or two, or three), you worry, and rightly so, that the noise will bother your neighbors. Certainly the sound of an insistently cackling hen is not pretty or melodic. If you happen to have a chicken that vocalizes in the morning, you can keep the coop dark (and the inhabitants asleep) until a reasonable hour. But most noisy hens are noisy all day. Fences and screening with sound-absorbing landscaping plants make for good neighbors. The prudent thing to do is to site the coop under your bedroom window, not your neighbor's. Keeping the hens busy with compost and greens keeps their beaks pecking instead of talking. But, honestly, if you have a noisy hen, well, it'll be noisy. It helps to keep it in perspective. For example, Onyx isn't half as loud as my neighbor's lawn mower. Etheldred's voice can't drown out the sound of an idling FedEx truck. A neighbor's barking dog is as loud as Garnet (another noisy hen here). And if you have a hen like Marge, when she's gone it will be markedly quieter and you'll miss the hubbub.

Feeding Your Hens

Chickens are omnivores. That means they'll scarf down just about anything, or at least try to! I've seen a hen catch and slurp down a snake like spaghetti. I've seen a chicken snatch a toad by its leg and all of the other hens go in a boisterous chase after it, only in the end to discover that a toad is not tasty. Chickens also eat less exciting foods, like vegetables, fruits, flowers, and grass. They eat grains and seeds. They scratch the ground and find bugs and specks of things that we can't see. So the question isn't really what chickens eat, but what the right diet is for them.

In the nineteenth century, most chickens were barnyard scavengers. They hatched out under their mamas, who taught them to look for oats in the horse stalls and for bugs and greens in the garden. The farmwife tossed stale bread and kitchen scraps to the hens. Chickens destined for the table were fattened on sour milk. Sometimes in the winter they'd be given a handful of grain. This haphazard diet was enough to sustain them. Farmers were satisfied when a hen laid 100 eggs a year. But over time flocks became larger and more confined. Chicken breeders focused on the laying trait, and egg production rocketed. Even many of the old-fashioned "heritage" breeds found in today's backyard flocks produce more eggs than a typical hen from the nineteenth century. Nowadays, a hen in one's backyard might lay from 150 to 200 eggs, or more, per year. With the increase in egg production came an increase in the nutritional requirements of the flock.

Commercial laying hen pellets (or crumbles, which are the same thing but smaller) are designed for today's productive hens. Creating a daily egg is depleting. The pellets have the right proportion of protein, minerals, and energy. These pellets should make up the bulk of your flock's diet. Your chickens should have access to the pellets all day long. They should go to bed with full crops (the crop is the pouch in the throat where the food is first stored after it is swallowed). It takes more than 25 hours to create an egg. During the night, as the hen is sleeping, she is still building that egg. She gets the materials for making it from digesting food. If her digestive tract is empty, she can't make the egg. So let your hen eat what she wants from sunup to sundown.

Calcium is the main component of the eggshell, and even though commercial pellets contain this essential mineral, it's good to provide an additional source. Coarsely broken-up oyster shell (purchased at the feed store) is the most easily absorbed form (even better than finely ground). I put it in a rabbit feed hopper hung on a wall in the coop, which makes it readily accessible and prevents waste.

If those pellets are the only food offered, a standard-size hen will eat between ¼ and ⅓ pound of them a day. However, it's essential for backyard chickens to have a varied diet beyond a commercial ration. The easiest way for them to get the greens and the variety that they need is to let them roam— they'll find plenty to eat under bushes, in the grass, and in leaf piles in the woods. For those of us who live where there are severe winters, or who keep hens on small lots or have too many predators in the neighborhood to allow for free-ranging, we have to provide a varied diet in other ways.

Almost anything that you would put into a compost bin you can offer to your hens. Not all of that refuse is ideal for chickens, but if your flock is getting most of its food intake from commercial pellets, then it's unlikely that they'll overeat any one item in the compost pile. Hens will eat the good stuff (like carrot tops) and ignore the inedible (like orange peels). Certainly, chickens appreciate table scraps. Mine chortle with glee and come running when they see me approach with the pail from the kitchen. They'll eat most anything, from stale toast to soggy green beans. Some foods they won't eat; hens have personal preferences! Mine don't like raisins, and yet it's a favorite treat for a friend's flock. Contrary to what you might read out there, potato skins and eggplant aren't going to cause any harm. They're members of the nightshade family, which some people avoid (but I don't). Green spots on potatoes contain solanine, which is toxic, but only in very large quantities. If your chickens were only eating table scraps and discards from the garden, then they might be so hungry that they would overeat something that is potentially harmful. But in my opinion, if they have their fill of laying hen pellets, and if presented with a wide variety of foodstuffs, they won't get sick. There's only one item that I know of that is lethal to chickens, and that is avocado. Avocados contain persin, a fungicidal toxin that can cause heart failure in birds (but not other animals).

Although your chickens will consume almost all offerings from your kitchen with gusto, some foods are better than others. If you provide too many carbs, like bread and stale cereal, your hens will get fat and won't get enough protein. Also, it will upset their mineral balance and can lead to thin-shelled eggs. So despite their enthusiasm, dole out the baked goods judiciously. In the summer, you can toss all of your garden waste, including bug-damaged zucchini, weeds, and grubs, to your chickens. I don't give them grass clippings or long scallion stalks, as those can cause impacted crops. (This occurs when food compacts into a solid mass in the crop, blocking the passage of all food and water. It is a potentially lethal situation.)

Although you can offer almost anything to your flock, it's not a good idea to simply throw kitchen scraps and garden waste into the pen, as what they don't eat will turn the yard into a mess and might go moldy, which will make chickens sick. Some people sort through their compost pail, separating out foods for their hens. Even doing that, the hens will reject some of it and so it will need to be raked up and removed from their pen. This is too much trouble for me. I have another system. To keep everything tidy and healthy, I've built a compost bin in the chicken run, a C-shaped container made out of chicken wire and fence posts. The chickens go in and out through the bin's opening, but the bulk of the compost stays inside. All of my kitchen and garden scraps get tossed into this bin. What the hens don't eat gets churned into tiny bits and quickly turns into good dirt, which I use in my garden. It's an easy, practical, and healthy system.

In the winter, when the compost pile is frozen, the hens still need greens and something to keep them busy, so I hang cabbages inside the coop for rousing games of cabbage tetherball. I also put treats into suet feeders hung on the wall.

Treats for Hens

Feeding treats to chickens is fun. Unlike so many others in our lives, chickens are raucously grateful for the smallest of offerings. But I've seen a disturbing trend toward overindulgence in the feeding of backyard hens. You can make your chickens sick—or even kill them—with too many of the wrong treats. One food that chickens love is cracked corn. It's like candy to them. But it has little nutritional value. It's okay to give a handful in the winter when the weather is really cold, as they could use the extra calories, but otherwise it has no benefit. It quickly makes hens fat, which can lead to serious egg-laying glitches. So as much as your girls are gleeful about cracked corn, don't use it for feed except for in very small quantities.

On the other end of the spectrum, I am concerned about the overfeeding of mealworms. A small amount, like a tablespoon a day, is a fine treat. But I've seen and heard about people who toss fistfuls to their flocks. They're practically feeding their hens pure protein (mealworms are up around 50 percent protein, whereas laying hens require 16 percent). The chicken expert at my local feed store told me about hens dying from kidney failure due to being fed mealworms as the main part of their diet. Besides the health dangers, mealworms are very expensive. Yes, it's good for chickens to eat bugs—bugs that they have found themselves, that are hidden and living in things that the chickens are sorting through, like a fallen log or a leaf pile. A chicken should have to work for her treats, by scratching and exploring. Chickens need to eat over the course of a long day, not binge at one time. Giving a large handful of mealworms or corn to your hens is the exact opposite of what is best for them.

Hulled sunflower seeds are a nice treat in moderation. They provide an extra bit of protein and also contain good essential fats. My retired girls, who are too old to forage, get about a teaspoon per bird per day. That's plenty! Don't feed the seeds with the shells on, as too many can cause an impacted crop. The sunflower seeds, and sometimes a small bit of cracked corn, are what I use to call my hens. All I have to do is put some in a cup and shake it. Since they rarely get such treats, when they hear that cup rattle, they know something very, very special is waiting for them.

You might see large, solid blocks of chicken treats at the feed store, which are supposed to be placed outside for foraging hens. These blocks attract chipmunks and mice to your run, and they don't encourage the hens to move about and search for food. They are also sweet, and so the hens prefer them to their pellets. If your girls are stuck indoors during the winter, a block can keep them busy. Otherwise, I don't think they're a good idea.

But all of this doesn't mean that you can't spoil your hens. One of the joys of chicken keeping is the happy commotion in the chicken yard when you bring out something special for them to eat. How wonderful that what is special to them can be a bruised tomato and cantaloupe seeds!

Water

The one most essential thing to provide your flock is fresh water. Even though it does seem as if chickens prefer muddy pools (rather like toddlers in rain puddles), always have clean water for them. Purchase a waterer designed for chickens. These gravity-fed founts hold up to several gallons of water. Put the water fount up off the ground (a few bricks work for this) so that it stays clean. Scrub it weekly with a plastic bristle brush. If algae blooms in the waterer, use a splash of white vinegar while cleaning, then rinse and fill. In the winter, if you are located in an area with freezing temperatures, either use an electric heating stand under the waterer (these are designed for chicken waterers) or be prepared to swap frozen waterers for fresh several times a day.

In the summer, I put an extra waterer out in the pen near the shady area where the hens like to hang out. Chickens overheat easily, and water will go a long way toward keeping them healthy and alive.

Pecking Order

The pecking order is the most basic of chicken behaviors. It's the way that a flock establishes hierarchy. Status determines who gets the best tidbit and who gets to sleep in the prime roosting spot. As the term implies, hens use their beaks to communicate dominance. But that doesn't mean that chickens spend their days attacking each other. A group of hens will quickly reach an agreement as to who is on top, and so on further down to the hen at the bottom of the social ladder. Despite the fact that chickens have no qualms about bossing underlings around, once the pecking order is set, the flock should be peaceful, with no obvious bullying.

It is personality, not size, that determines who is the queen hen. I've found that the breeds that are the most active foragers, such as Barred Plymouth Rocks, Wyandottes, and Rhode Island Reds, tend to be the dominant ones, while the Welsummers, Cochins, and Delawares are lower down. But there are always exceptions. I had a bantam White Leghorn who ruled the barnyard. She was an active and scrappy bird whose personality made up for her diminutive size.

Hens that have been raised together as chicks rarely have issues. They've figured out who's on top from early on. As the pullets mature, there might be a few tiffs as a hen grows larger and bolder, but there shouldn't be anything dramatic or bloody. As much as it's called "pecking order," the hens have all sorts of other body language that they use before they resort to stabbing each other with their pointy beaks. Besides all that, low-status birds are smart enough to get out of the way.

If there are frequent squabbles in your flock, or if a hen is getting bloodied, then you have a management issue. The most common reason for pecking-order violence is crowding. Even if it looks like you've provided enough space, be aware that there are times when the chickens won't be spread out evenly. Take a look at your hens' accommodations during inclement weather. Are they crammed together? Sometimes reorganizing the coop can relieve the pressure. Adding outside roosts will give lower-status hens a place to go, or conversely, a perch from which the high-status hens can survey their realm. Chickens are greedy and possessive about food. Hang the feeder so that the hens can circle around it and no one gets trapped in a corner while eating. Add a second waterer outside. Provide treats in several places.

Chickens get bored, and hens kept in small dirt pens will peck at each other to relieve tension. I have a number of tricks to keep my hens out of trouble. I put a log in the run, which I move every few days. Underneath it the hens find bugs to eat, and as the log falls apart the hens peck at it. I also have a compost pile in the run that provides plenty of interesting things to eat and scratch at. I give them pumpkins in the fall, and in the summer I toss clods of dirt and weeds into their pen. In the winter I hang cabbages and greens in the coop.

There are times when the pecking order is upset, and when that happens what goes on can take you aback—chest thumping, feather pulling, blood letting! In the worst-case scenario, a picked-on hen will be severely injured or even killed by the others.

Some people ascribe all sorts of bad intentions to the offending "bullies," but in truth the animals are not at fault, for their behavior is a result of how we manage their care.

If you notice a sudden increase in aggression in your flock, look for a cause. Sometimes it's a change in one chicken's health. Chickens recognize each other by their combs, and a change in a comb's color (which can happen at the onset of illness, before you notice something is wrong) will set the others off. Bullying can also be incited by an injury. If a chicken is wounded, and especially if there's blood, she'll become a target of the entire flock. If the injury isn't severe, darken the exposed skin with Blu-Kote (a purple antiseptic); if it's open and bloody, remove her from the group until she's healed.

Pecking order is always disturbed when new chickens are introduced. It can be especially difficult adding one young pullet to an established flock of hens. During a normal bit of sorting out, there will be chest thumping and running at each other. This can go on for days, but things will quiet down. Sometimes the attacks seem endless, and they can be severe. I've seen one hen jump on another's back to pin her down and fiercely peck at the head. Chickens doing that can kill. Roosters don't allow this sort of hen-on-hen attack, stopping it by interrupting the behavior. This is something that you can do, too. Sometimes all it takes is for you to pick up the bully and move her away from the hen that she is focused on. Do this a half a dozen times and she usually ends up getting the message. Also effective is to calmly walk between the two fighting hens to separate them. Don't try to fix things by hitting the offending hen. That doesn't communicate to her that she needs to cease her attacks.

Once in a while there is a hen that is an unrelenting bully. Reform her by removing her from the flock, out of sight, for four days. I have a spare rabbit hutch behind the barn that I use for this purpose. It takes two to three days for the other hens to establish a new pecking order without the bully. You want that to settle down before reintroducing the hen. When returned to the flock, she will be at the bottom of the pecking order and will rarely go back to her aggressive ways.

A flock of hens that all get along is a pleasure to have in the backyard. But keep in mind that under their cheerful clucking, the pecking order is always simmering. If you pay attention to your hens' behavior, health, and resources, it won't boil over, and you'll all be happy.

Predators and Vermin

There are many predators, in both the countryside and the city, that want a chicken dinner. There are also vermin that want your flock's food. These animals must be taken into account when designing and maintaining your hens' home. It is not true that if you have chickens you'll also have predators like coyotes circling your property and rats invading your lawn, though those animals will stop by to see whether they can get in. If your coop and pen are fenced and the feed is stored properly, then the predators will recognize that your birds are unattainable and the vermin will find easier pickings elsewhere. (They won't hang around once they figure out that they're not getting a chicken dinner.)

Large predators that kill chickens include foxes, coyotes, fisher cats, raccoons, opossums, bears, weasels, and bobcats. But it is not only wild animals that are a danger to your flock. An unleashed pet dog can be the worst predator and will gleefully kill all of your chickens in minutes. In the South, black snakes and skunks eat eggs out of the nesting boxes. If you're a chicken, it's a dangerous world out there! But, fences and a secure coop can keep the predators at bay.

Meshed fencing, like chicken wire with openings no larger than 1-inch square, is best for containing and protecting your flock. Install it at least 6 inches underground to deter burrowing animals. If you are able to let your chickens range freely, then consider moveable electric net fencing that allows you to protect your flock while rotating the pasture that they forage on.

Overhead there is danger from hawks, eagles, and owls. In my backyard, there is a nesting pair of red-tailed hawks, so I only let my hens out to free-range when I am outside and watching them. If there are raptors in your neighborhood, attach wire or flexible netting (sold as "hawk netting") above the permanent pen. Fencing, though, will not protect your flock at night. I learned the truth of this after a raccoon climbed the fence, ripped off the hawk netting, and then entered the henhouse and killed my chickens. I now lock my birds in at night (from the inside, as raccoons can open some latches). Window and door screens are not sturdy enough to keep predators out; use hardware cloth.

Mice and rats are the bane of chicken keepers. At the least they eat the food, and at most the rats will eat eggs and kill hens. Also, vermin are disease vectors. These rodents use tunnels for ingress and egress. This is one reason why I have concrete floors in my coops. Another option is to have a wood floor and raise the coop up off the ground on blocks to prevent the animals from tunneling in.

Also, discourage rodents from nesting in your coop by keeping it tidy and clean. Raking the outside pen and keeping it as packed dirt instead of deep litter will remove the vermin's ability to burrow and approach the coop. I do this at least once a week. Storing all feed bags and treats in galvanized metal cans will dissuade vermin from taking up residence. If you notice a rodent problem, then remove the hanging feeder at night and store it in a metal can, as rats feed in the dark when the chickens sleep. These pests are in everyone's neighborhoods; what you don't want is to become their feeding station. With attentive management of the coop and run they will ignore your property and go elsewhere.

Chicken Care in Cold Weather

A hen has about 8,500 feathers. That makes for a warm coat. Like her wild bird cousins, she fluffs up to trap air under her down, which will keep her cozy, even in below-freezing temperatures. However, a sharp, cold wind that ruffles the feathers will make her shiver. Icy rain on the hen's head and mud frozen on her legs will chill her to the bone. So although that fine-feathered garment can keep a hen plenty warm even in the coldest weather, there are some things to do to keep her comfortable and healthy when the winter storms hit.

Cold isn't the problem; damp is. Moisture in the air and wet bedding can lead to illness in your flock. Manure is mostly water, and in the winter, when the coop is closed up, the windows will be coated with a sheen of ice, and the air will be heavy with moisture. Manure also contains nitrogen, which gives off ammonia gas as it breaks down. The moisture and ammonia make the hens prone to respiratory disease. Although chickens need shelter that is out of the wind and free of drafts, a closed-up barn can be harmful to their health, and so good ventilation is a must. Vents near the eaves provide airflow without drafts. I have cupolas on my coops that keep the air circulating and dry year-round. Keeping the coop mucked out and bedded with absorbent pine shavings also helps to keep the flock healthy.

Most chickens do not need heat lamps; in fact, a heater can do more harm than good. Hens that huddle under a heat lamp will not fluff out their feathers, so when they move away from the heat to eat or roost, they'll be cold. They might not leave the heater to eat or exercise. It's not good for them to go from one extreme temperature to another. I keep my chickens in uninsulated, unheated coops through New England winters, when temperatures can go weeks without rising above freezing, and my hens have been fine. Coops in more extreme climates, like Alaska, do benefit from insulation and heat. But in those places the hens don't go outside at all.

A few breeds are not cold hardy, but even those don't require heat. Frizzles have feathers that are twisted and that don't repel rain and snow, and so those birds can get wet to the bone. Silkies' feathers are soft like down and look like fur. They also absorb water like a sponge. In the winter the damp cold can kill them, so it's essential that these birds stay dry. Keep them indoors or in covered runs. Also, some hens, and more often roosters, have big combs, prone to frostbite. Slather some petroleum jelly on them if you know the temperature is going to drop.

Chickens don't like walking on snow or ice, but they do like to be outside, even in freezing temperatures. So take a moment and shovel a clear area for them in their run. Or, if the snow is too deep and icy, put down some hay. They'll appreciate a spot that is high and dry. If your run gets muddy, add a few bags of coarse sand to give the hens a place to roam above the muck.

One of the most important things to do in the winter is to give your chickens free-flowing water. A hen without fresh water can die in two days. One solution is to buy several founts, and when one freezes, swap it with a fresh one. It's not enough to leave water early in the morning and then come home at night and provide fresh water again then. Chickens can't see in the dark, and so your hens won't make use of that nighttime water. Electricity in the coop makes the winter much easier, as you can put the waterer on a heated base (specifically made for coops and widely available).

In the winter, the flock's feed ration needs a bit of adjustment. Chickens don't have as much forage in the winter, so they'll likely eat more pellets. You can toss them some scratch grains in the bedding to keep them busy and give them a calorie boost. Greens and other vegetables are as important in the winter as they are in the summer. In addition to hanging cabbages and providing pumpkins, I nail a wild bird suet feeder on a wall inside the coop, and I use it to hold treats like a slice of bread, apple halves, and kale leaves. It takes effort to peck at these foods, and it keeps the girls busy all day.

Chicken Care in Hot Weather

People who have had chickens for years know that it's the heat you worry about, not the cold. You know that the hens are struggling when they have their beaks open and are panting. You know they're in trouble when they are listless and not drinking. Chickens can die from heat stroke. Fortunately, there are things that you can do for your hens to alleviate heat stress so that you don't have to bring them into your air-conditioned living room.

First of all, chickens must have shade. If you can't site your coop under trees, put an awning up. Provide a shady area with loose dirt where the hens can wallow down in cool soil. Also, keep a waterer in the shade. If it's really hot, the hens won't go across the sunny ground to get to the fount in the coop. I know people who live in seriously hot places, like central Texas, who provide misters for their chickens, and they cool off their coops by spraying water on them. That's not necessary where I live, but I do hose down the dirt in the pen when the temperature gets over 90°F.

I always have a chicken or two that go broody in the worst of the heat and insist on staying inside the stuffy coop, inside of an even stuffier metal nesting box. After having no success getting them to go somewhere more comfortable, I've finally given up and hung an old box fan to blow air on them.

Hot weather is so stressful for hens that their egg production suffers during heat spells. Keeping your hens comfortable in the summer takes a bit of extra attention and work, but your hens will appreciate it, and you'll get the added benefit of more eggs.

Chickens and Your Garden

Chickens are beautiful animals, and when we first bring them home, we imagine that they will be like moving garden ornaments, decorating our vegetable plots and lawn. But, the truth is that, if not managed, hens are actively destructive forces in our yards. There are two things that chickens do all day long: scratch and eat. They have strong legs with sharp claws, and they use them to kick up dirt, looking for yummy tidbits, until there is no grass left. Chickens are omnivores, so although it's true that they eat insect pests, they also peck at anything that looks edible, and will down your seedlings, sunflowers, and tomatoes, among other plants both beautiful and useful. One hen can clean all the fruit off of a raspberry bush in minutes! While they're foraging, they'll leave piles of stinky manure everywhere. They like sitting on lawn chairs and will claim them for their own. They also like to dust-bathe, and scratch up turf and garden for their spa sessions. Let your flock loose on a daily basis in your garden, and your garden will soon be reduced to bare earth, dust wallows, and decimated plants.

However, managed properly, chickens can be a boon to the garden. I let my hens into the vegetable plot in the spring and fall, when they eat up the overwintered grubs and turn the dirt over, readying it for planting. During the growing season, they are kept out by good fencing. They are still helpful at this time because I toss them the vegetables ruined by pests, as well as plants no longer producing, which they devour and turn into manure. This manure is raked up, composted, and put back into the garden, where it helps the garden grow.

Despite what my hens do to the yard, I do like to let them free-range. I don't expect my garden to be perfect, so a bit of scratching and pecking at established perennials is fine with me. Their forays are always under my watchful eye; while I protect my tender plants from the chickens, I also protect the hens from predators (hawks are a constant threat in my neighborhood). I enjoy seeing the girls enjoy their outings. Sitting on a lawn chair, lemonade in hand, watching happy, chortling hens milling about the yard, is one of the great pleasures of chicken keeping.

The Recipes

Scrambled Eggs

Farmstead eggs are so delicious that even the simplest of preparations makes for a satisfying meal. Cooking doesn't get any easier than scrambling up a few eggs. Some people swear by adding extra yolks and cream, but I think that the beauty of scrambled eggs is in how simple they are. The flavor and color of eggs from backyard hens don't need any additions. That said, if your idea of the perfect scrambled eggs is a very soft dish, then add a splash of milk or cream to the beaten eggs before cooking. Scrambled eggs and toast are a classic breakfast, but don't limit their enjoyment to the morning. A favorite dinner in my house is scrambled eggs, smoked salmon, toast, and a salad.

Scrambled Eggs

For perfect scrambled eggs you don't need anything other than really good fresh eggs and butter. How incredibly delicious just two ingredients—eggs and butter—can be! Sure, you can cook up scrambled eggs in a nonstick pan spritzed with cooking spray, but give yourself a treat and use real butter. Finish off with good sea salt, or dust with one of my seasoned salt recipes (page 79). Scrambled eggs should be soft and pillowy, yet not watery. When cooked too quickly over high heat, the proteins in the whites tighten up and squeeze out the water inherent in the eggs, so don't rush it! Set the pan over medium-low heat and move the eggs with a spatula until they cook up into mounds of delicious and moist curds. This recipe can be doubled and still be prepared in a 10-inch skillet. However, don't cook more than 8 eggs at a time in a 10-inch skillet or some of the eggs will overcook as the rest are setting. A larger pan can of course handle more eggs, but make sure it is a heavy skillet that radiates heat evenly.

Once cooked, scrambled eggs should be served immediately. Eggs at restaurant buffets are often prepared from "whole liquid eggs with color stabilizer," which is why they can be left in a chafing dish for hours. Your eggs at home won't last like that, thank goodness.

Makes 2 servings

1 tablespoon unsalted butter

4 large eggs

Kosher salt

1. Heat a 10-inch skillet over low heat and melt the butter until it just begins to bubble but doesn't brown.

2. Whisk the eggs and then pour them into the pan. Using a rubber spatula, stir frequently, pushing the eggs from the center to the sides of the pan so that raw egg moves into contact with the hot skillet. Serve as soon as the eggs firm up. Add salt to taste.

Scrambled Eggs with Sausage, Cheddar, and Peppers

Imagine a leisurely Sunday morning reading the paper. No pressure to do anything or go anywhere. Now imagine that scene with a plate of these scrambled eggs in front of you, plus toast, orange juice, and a mug of strong coffee on the side. Some of the best things in life can be had right at home.

Makes 4 servings

8 ounces sausage (breakfast or Italian-style)

1 cup chopped bell peppers (use a combination of green, red, and yellow)

1 tablespoon unsalted butter

6 large eggs

2 tablespoons milk

½ cup grated sharp cheddar cheese

1. Remove the sausage from the casing and break it into pieces. Cook in a nonstick skillet or well-seasoned cast-iron pan over medium heat until browned. Transfer to a plate.

2. If using pork sausages, there will be a lot of grease in the skillet. Pour it out so that only a thin coating remains. If using low-fat chicken sausage, you might have to add some of the butter in order to sauté the peppers. Add the peppers to the pan and cook over medium heat until softened. Set the peppers aside with the sausage.

3. Melt the butter in the pan. Whisk the eggs and milk together. Pour the eggs into the pan. Stir occasionally until the eggs are half-set. Add the sausage and peppers. Cook until softly set.

4. Stir in the cheese. Cook briefly, until the cheese begins to melt.

Bombay Scrambled Eggs

Scrambled eggs don't have to be plain or eaten only at breakfast. In India, scrambled eggs are studded with onions, herbs, and spices. I've specified jalapeño peppers here because they are moderately spicy and are easy to find in the market, but you can use any of a number of fresh hot chile peppers. Try this as a sandwich filling in a pita pocket.

Makes 4 servings

2 tablespoons vegetable oil

1 cup chopped onion

1 clove garlic, minced

6 large eggs

½ teaspoon kosher salt

¼ teaspoon freshly ground black pepper

½ teaspoon ground cumin

1 fresh jalapeño, seeded and minced

2 tablespoons chopped fresh cilantro

1. Heat the oil in a large nonstick skillet or well-seasoned cast-iron pan over low heat. Sauté the onion and garlic until very soft and golden.

2. In a bowl, whisk the eggs, salt, pepper, cumin, and jalapeño together. Pour this into the skillet. Stir and cook until the eggs are firm but not dry. Stir in 1 tablespoon of the cilantro. Serve garnished with the remaining cilantro.

Matzo Brei

During Passover, an eight-day Jewish holiday, Jews don't consume leavened bread but do eat matzo, a flat, dry cracker. For breakfast, instead of scrambled eggs and toast, we often have matzo brei. Looking at this recipe, you might wonder, why bother? The ingredients—bland crackers, eggs, salt, and butter—don't look that interesting. But all together they are! The texture of crackers and eggs fried up in a skillet is perfect. This is one scrambled egg recipe that is done over a higher heat in order to crisp the edges of the egg-soaked matzo. Feel free to multiply to serve more people. Matzo brei is seasoned generously with salt, which is then balanced with jam or sugar—or both.

Makes 1 serving

1 matzo

1 large egg

¼ teaspoon kosher salt

1 tablespoon unsalted butter
  or vegetable oil

Jam or granulated sugar, for serving

1. Break the matzo into large pieces over a colander in the sink. Pour cold water over the pieces for about 30 seconds. Let drain, and then squeeze the excess water out of the crackers. This will crumble the matzo but shouldn't turn it to mush.

2. In a medium bowl, beat the egg with a fork. Stir in the salt. Stir in the moistened matzo.

3. Heat the butter in a nonstick skillet or well-seasoned cast-iron pan over medium heat, a little hotter than you would cook scrambled eggs because you want the edges of the matzo to crisp. Wait until the butter melts and begins to foam, and then add the egg and matzo mixture. Cook, stirring occasionally to break up the eggs. Serve immediately with jam or sugar.

Vegetable Fried Rice

Scrambled eggs are an essential ingredient in fried rice. What would this dish be without those small bits of rich, soft yellow eggs? This version is just right for a light supper. For a heartier meal, in the final step add ½ cup diced cooked chicken or ham or shrimp, or all three. The best rice for fried rice is cooked rice that has cooled and dried out a bit. Leftover rice from a Chinese restaurant is ideal.

Makes 2 servings

4 cups cooked white rice

3 large eggs

2 teaspoons dry sherry

¼ cup chopped scallions

1 rib celery, chopped

¼ cup diced carrot

½ cup peas (thawed if frozen)

1 cup diced vegetables of your choice

3 tablespoons vegetable oil

½ teaspoon kosher salt

¼ teaspoon freshly ground
   black pepper

1 tablespoon soy sauce

1. Separate the rice grains with your fingers and set aside in a bowl.

2. In a small bowl, mix the eggs and sherry until combined. Place the scallions, celery, carrots, peas, and diced vegetables in another bowl.

3. Heat a wok or a large skillet over medium heat. Pour in 2 tablespoons of the oil. Add the eggs and stir constantly until scrambled and broken into small lumps.

4. Stir in the rice and cook until the eggs and rice are evenly distributed throughout.

5. Increase the heat, add the remaining 1 tablespoon oil, and add the vegetables, salt, pepper, and soy sauce. Cook until the vegetables are just cooked and heated through.

Spaghetti alla Carbonara

Like Fettuccine Alfredo (page 60), the eggs here are cooked not in a pan, but by the hot pasta. However, unlike that recipe, this one uses whole eggs and doesn't require cream. It does use pancetta, which is an Italian bacon that isn't smoked or sweetened like American bacon. If you can't find it, substitute your favorite bacon.

Makes 4 large servings

1 pound spaghetti

3 large eggs

¼ cup grated Romano cheese

½ cup grated Parmesan cheese, plus more for serving

1 tablespoon olive oil

8 ounces pancetta, cut into ½-inch dice

2 cloves garlic, smashed and peeled

½ teaspoon kosher salt

2 tablespoons sliced fresh basil

¼ teaspoon freshly ground black pepper

1. Bring a large pot of generously salted water to a boil. Cook the pasta according to the package directions.

2. While the pasta is cooking, crack the eggs into a large, shallow serving bowl. Whisk to break up the egg yolks. Stir in the cheeses.

3. Also while the pasta is cooking, heat the olive oil in a skillet over medium heat. Add the pancetta and garlic. Cook until the pancetta is crispy. Discard the garlic.

4. As soon as the pasta is done, drain it in a colander. Shake a few times to remove the excess water, then put it in the bowl with the eggs and cheese, and toss. The hot pasta will cook the eggs.

5. Add the pancetta with the olive oil to the pasta. Stir in the salt and garnish with the basil. Sprinkle the pepper on top. Serve immediately with additional Parmesan.

Fettuccine Alfredo with Rosemary and Garlic

When I worked the lunch line at a little bistro, I loved it when an order for fettuccine Alfredo came through. It was so easy and absolutely foolproof. If you think about it, the sauce is like rich scrambled eggs cooked by the heat of the fettuccine. At this bistro, the head chef was German, and we did an untraditional version with a lot of garlic. The rosemary is my addition. I think it needs that pungent bit of herb to balance the rich cream.

Makes 4 servings

1 pound fettuccine

4 tablespoons (½ stick) unsalted butter

2 cloves garlic, minced

1 cup heavy cream

1 cup grated Parmesan cheese, plus more for garnish

3 egg yolks

½ teaspoon kosher salt

¼ teaspoon freshly ground black pepper

1 tablespoon chopped fresh rosemary

1. Bring a large pot of generously salted water to a boil and cook the fettuccine according to the package directions.

2. Meanwhile, heat 1 tablespoon of the butter over low heat in a medium sauté pan. Add the garlic and cook for several minutes. Add the remaining 3 tablespoons butter and cook until melted.

3. Pour in ¾ cup of the cream and add the cheese. Cook, stirring frequently, for 2 minutes or until thickened.

4. In a small bowl, whisk the egg yolks, the remaining ¼ cup cream, salt, and pepper.

5. When the pasta is done, immediately drain it into a large colander. Shake a few times to remove the excess water, then put it into a pasta serving bowl (a large, shallow bowl). Pour in the cream and cheese mixture and then stir in the egg yolk mixture. Toss quickly so that the pasta is thoroughly coated and the yolks cook.

6. Toss in the rosemary and top with additional Parmesan.

Fried Eggs

There are three styles of fried eggs: sunny side up, over easy, and over hard. How you like your eggs is a personal choice. Whichever way you prefer them, you'll notice a difference when you fry one from a farmstead. Crack a commercial egg and it spreads out thinly, often more than 6 inches across. Crack a farmstead egg and the whites are thick and the yolk stands up tall. This makes quite a difference in cooking, because a thin egg will overcook and toughen in the skillet. On the other hand, a farmstead egg will take longer to set and will end up firm yet not rubbery.

Fried Eggs

A secret to perfectly cooked eggs is to keep the heat low. Low temperatures allow the egg to solidify without losing moisture. This rule is especially true for fried eggs. Even the butter for fried eggs should be melted in the skillet over low heat so that it bubbles but doesn't brown.

Using fat to grease the pan makes a difference. You can fry an egg in a nonstick skillet and slip it off with a spatula, but without grease, that egg will look like a plastic toy from a play set. Butter adds flavor and moisture. You don't need much. Some people do prefer fried eggs with thin, crispy edges. If you are in that group, then use vegetable oil and a slightly higher temperature. I like fried eggs both ways, but I think that the best fried eggs are those eaten on a camping trip, cooked in bacon grease over a hot camp stove.

Makes 2 eggs

Unsalted butter

2 large eggs

Sunny Side Up

These eggs are picture-perfect. The whites are bright, with none of the browning that comes from flipping the egg over, and the spherical yolks look like little suns (hence the name).

1. Melt enough butter over low heat to coat the pan generously (a heavy nonstick pan is best).

2. Crack the egg into the pan and cover with a lid.

3. Cook for 3 to 4 minutes, until the outer yolk firms up but the center remains soft and a touch runny.

Over Easy

1. Melt the butter in a skillet over medium-low heat.

2. Crack the egg into the pan and cook until the white is done all the way but the yolk is still runny, about 1 minute. Use a spatula to flip the egg over.

3. Cook for 1 to 2 minutes more, until the edges of the yolk begin to solidify but the inside remains soft.

Over Hard

These eggs are for those who don't like runny yolks. The trick here is to set the yolk without having the white turn tough and rubbery.

1. Cook the same way as for over easy, making sure the temperature is quite low.

2. Once you've flipped the egg, keep cooking until the yolk is thoroughly set, about 3 minutes.

Birdie in a Basket

One of my earliest memories is of eating birdie in a basket. Frying an egg in a hole torn out of a piece of bread is a whimsical, appealing way to serve eggs. As a child, I never would have eaten a lone fried egg, but I happily ate a birdie in a basket whenever it was put in front of me. Use your favorite bread here.

Makes 1 serving

Unsalted butter

1 slice bread

1 egg

Kosher salt and freshly ground
    black pepper

1. Generously butter the bread on both sides. Tear or cut a hole from the center of the bread or use a cookie cutter, such as a heart shape, to cut out the "basket."

2. Heat a skillet over medium heat and add just enough butter to coat the surface. Put in the slice of bread and then crack the egg into the hole. Cook until the bottom sets and the bread toasts. Turn over and continue to cook to the desired doneness.

3. Slip the bread and egg onto a plate. If you used a cookie cutter, fry the cutout center piece, too, and set it next to the egg on the plate. Serve with salt and pepper.

Fried Egg Breakfast Sandwich

This recipe is just what a fried egg sandwich should be. In quality, flavor, and texture it is nothing like the fast-food version. It takes no more time to prepare than it does to drive through a take-out window at rush hour, so do make your own! It's a recipe to be creative with: Try leftover aioli spread on the English muffin, or use sliced tomato and mozzarella cheese instead of the bacon and cheddar.

Makes 1 serving

1 to 2 teaspoons unsalted butter, as needed

1 large egg

1 English muffin

Kosher salt and freshly ground black pepper

1 slice Canadian bacon

1 slice cheddar cheese

1. Melt the butter in a nonstick or well-seasoned cast-iron skillet over medium-low heat. Use enough butter to coat the surface of the pan. Crack the egg into the skillet and cook until the egg white sets and the yolk begins to firm, about 2 minutes.

2. Flip the egg over and cook until the yolk is thoroughly set, about 3 minutes more. At the same time, toast the English muffin. When the muffin is toasted, set the egg on the bottom half. Add salt and pepper to taste.

3. Increase the heat and fry the bacon until one side browns. Turn it over and top with the cheese. When the bacon is cooked and the cheese has melted, use a spatula to slip it on top of the egg. Top with the other English muffin half.

Egg Panini

Don't pass this recipe by because it looks so basic. It is crazy good. Also, although a panini press will make the sandwiches look professional, that specialized appliance isn't necessary. A large skillet with a heavy bottom, so that the heat radiates evenly, is all that it takes to make a perfect pressed sandwich.

Makes 1 serving

2 tablespoons unsalted butter

2 slices hearty bread

1 tablespoon mayonnaise (page 140, or use store-bought)

½ ripe avocado, thinly sliced

3 slices ripe tomato

2 slices sharp cheddar cheese

1 cooked-through fried egg (page 63)

1. Heat a heavy skillet (use cast iron if you have it) over medium heat, or preheat a panini press. Butter one side of each slice of bread. Spread the mayonnaise on the other side.

2. Construct the sandwich by layering on the remaining ingredients.

3. Place the sandwich in the skillet (or the panini press) and heat through until the cheese begins to melt and the bread toasts. Turn over and continue to cook, pressing down a few times, until the cheese is oozing.

Croque Madame

This sandwich is a grilled ham and cheese topped with a fried egg and tangy greens, meant to be eaten with a fork. The ingredients are simple, but when they are of the best quality, this sandwich reaches the next level of deliciousness.

Makes 1 sandwich

Salted butter as needed

2 slices rustic, sturdy bread

Stone-ground mustard as needed

2 slices Swiss cheese

1 slice ham

1 large egg

Kosher salt and freshly ground
   black pepper

¼ cup tangy greens, like watercress

1. Butter one side of each slice of bread, and spread mustard on the other side.

2. Heat a heavy skillet over medium heat. Put one slice of bread buttered side down, layer on the cheese and ham, and then top with the second slice of bread. Cook as you would a grilled cheese sandwich, slowly so that the cheese melts. Turn over once the bread toasts on the first side.

3. Meanwhile, fry the egg sunny-side up (page 62). Generously season with salt and pepper.

4. Top the cooked sandwich with the egg and then the greens.

Huevos Rancheros

I don't claim that these are totally authentic huevos rancheros, but they are delicious and very easy to make. However, *queso fresco* is an authentically south-of-the-border ingredient. It's a delicious salty, tart, and dry Mexican cheese. It's worth a trip to a cheese store to find it. Feta is similar and would also be good here.

Makes 1 serving

2 tablespoons salsa of your choice

2 teaspoons vegetable oil, or
  as needed

1 large egg

One 5-inch corn tortilla

1 tablespoon grated queso fresco

1. Heat the salsa in a small saucepan or the microwave until hot but not bubbling. Keep warm.

2. Pour enough of the oil into a small cast-iron or nonstick skillet to lightly coat the surface. Over medium heat, fry the egg until it is as firm as desired. Transfer to a plate.

3. Heating a tortilla in oil can be tricky. The goal is to have a warm, pliable base for the egg. Too little oil and the tortilla will be tough; too much and it will be greasy. It also must be eaten right away, so cook the tortilla after you've fried the egg. Heat about 1 teaspoon of oil in the skillet over medium-high heat. As soon as the tortilla buckles, turn it over and cook the other side. Immediately put the tortilla on a plate. Place the egg in the center, spoon on the salsa, and top with the cheese.

Fried Eggs and Goat Cheese

This is my favorite summer dinner. In the late afternoon, most of the hens have laid their eggs and are busy outside. When it's time for supper, I step out the back porch door. I go to the garden and grab a tomato and some herbs. Usually there are a few damaged cherry tomatoes that have fallen to the ground. I pick those up, too, and toss them to the hens. The girls run after them, and I go into the coop and collect the gifts that they've left in the nesting boxes. I head back to the house, and dinner is soon ready.

Makes 2 servings

2 tablespoons dried bread crumbs

½ teaspoon kosher salt

2 ounces goat cheese, crumbled (⅓ cup)

2 teaspoons olive oil, or as needed

1 large tomato, diced

¼ cup sliced fresh basil

1 tablespoon chopped fresh parsley

4 large eggs

1. Combine the bread crumbs, salt, and goat cheese in a small bowl.

2. Pour enough of the olive oil into a large nonstick pan to coat the surface. Sauté the tomato, basil, and parsley until the tomato is soft but not mushy. Set aside in a bowl.

3. If necessary, add a touch more olive oil to the pan. Crack the eggs into the pan and top with the cheese mixture. Cook over medium-low heat until the egg whites set. Using a spatula, separate the eggs and flip them (and the cheese mixture) over. Top with the sautéed tomatoes. Cook until the yolks are as firm as desired.

Steak and Eggs with Shallot-Garlic Butter and Sweet Onions

Cooking steak and eggs is fun. My favorite steak here is a boneless rib eye, but use whatever looks good at the market. I make this in a big cast-iron skillet. The meat sizzles, and the onions and peppers create a mouthwatering aroma. The eggs are fried last in the pan, and they absorb the juices from the meat and vegetables. I imagine myself at a chuck wagon stove with stars overhead. On summer nights we eat this on the porch and, if lucky, watch the lightning bugs put on a show.

Makes 4 servings

One 1-pound steak, 1 inch thick

Kosher salt and freshly ground
   black pepper

1 to 2 tablespoons vegetable oil

1 green bell pepper, sliced

1 clove garlic, sliced

1 sweet onion, such as Vidalia, sliced

1 tablespoon Shallot-Garlic Butter
   (recipe follows)

4 large eggs

1. Rub the steak with salt and pepper. Heat a large skillet and pour in enough oil to thoroughly coat the bottom. A cast-iron skillet is perfect for this sort of recipe, although a large, heavy-bottomed pan will do. Cook the steak for 5 to 7 minutes on each side, until done as desired.

2. While the steak is cooking, surround it with the bell pepper, garlic, and onion slices. Cook the vegetables until very soft and golden (about the same time as it takes the steak to cook).

3. Transfer the vegetables to a serving platter and cover with aluminum foil to keep warm. Transfer the steak to a cutting board. Top the steak with slices of the shallot-garlic butter and let it rest while cooking the eggs.

4. Fry the eggs in the skillet according to your preference.

5. Slice the steak and put it on the serving plate with the vegetables. Set the eggs on the side.

Shallot-Garlic Butter

1 clove garlic, peeled

½ teaspoon kosher salt

1 tablespoon minced shallot

1 tablespoon minced fresh parsley

4 tablespoons unsalted butter,
   softened

1. Using the flat side of a chef's knife, smash the garlic with the salt, and then mince until it becomes a paste.

2. Stir the garlic paste, shallot, and parsley into the butter. Put the butter on a piece of plastic wrap, shape it into a narrow log, wrap tightly, and refrigerate for up to 1 week or freeze for up to 2 months. Use extra on grilled fish or to sauté vegetables.

Angel Hair Pasta with Fried Eggs

Topping garlicky angel hair pasta with fried eggs elevates this recipe from a side dish to a main course. It's so good and easy that it will become your weeknight "I don't have time and I don't know what to eat" go-to recipe. For a light version, substitute cooked spaghetti squash for the pasta.

Makes 4 servings

8 ounces angel hair pasta

4 tablespoons olive oil

1 large shallot, minced

2 cloves garlic, minced

1 cup cherry tomatoes, halved, or chopped large tomatoes

2 tablespoons chopped fresh basil

4 large eggs

Sea salt and freshly ground black pepper

¼ cup grated Parmesan cheese

1. Bring a large pot of generously salted water to a boil. Cook the pasta according to the directions on the package. Drain and put into a serving bowl. Keep warm.

2. Heat the oil in a sauté pan. Cook the shallot and garlic until softened and golden. Add the tomatoes and cook until they wilt.

3. Add the vegetables to the drained pasta. Using a rubber spatula, scrape in most of the oil. Toss, add the basil, and toss again.

4. Fry the eggs in the same pan that you used to cook the vegetables. There should be enough remaining oil, but if not, add a touch more. Dust the eggs with salt and pepper.

5. Divide the pasta among plates. Set an egg on each. Top with the cheese.

Hard- and Soft-Cooked Eggs

A much-relied-on pantry staple in my refrigerator is a bowl of peeled, hard-cooked eggs. My teenage son often grabs one on the way out the door to catch the school bus. Midmorning, when I need something to eat to keep me going, I'll eat a hard-cooked egg dipped in some seasoned salt. When lunchtime comes around, it takes only a minute to make egg salad. Hard-cooked eggs are the base of some of my favorite recipes, like Classic Deviled Eggs (page 83; who doesn't love them?) and Beef and Egg Piroshki (page 91).

The shells peel easily off of hard-cooked supermarket eggs, but not off fresh farmstead eggs. That's because commercial eggs have gone through a hot water and chemical wash before storage, and then they are days to weeks old before purchase. This loosens the membrane that separates the egg from the shell. An egg from one of your own hens is so fresh that the whites stick to the shell and you end up tossing half of the white along with the shell. There's an easy solution to this quandary. Simply set aside some in a carton for 10 days. They'll still be fresh and delicious when hard-cooked, but they'll also shed their peels without a fuss. If you can't wait that long, then use the steam-cooking method on the following page, which works because eggshells are porous: The steam penetrates the shell and that dislodges the membrane. However, you still have to have eggs a few days old for the steaming method to work.

Some people claim that all you have to do to easily peel hard-cooked fresh eggs is to boil them in water that has a touch of vinegar added to it. However, I don't like this option. Vinegar reacts chemically with the shell to break it down into calcium carbonate and gas. If you leave an egg in a bowl of vinegar for a day or more, the shell will dissolve. Leave it in long enough and the egg turns into a rubberized ball! (This was one of my son's favorite science experiments.) Not only do eggs boiled in vinegar have that vinegar odor, but also the texture of the white goes mushy.

One other thing that you do not have to do when hard-cooking eggs is to prick the ends of the eggs before cooking! I've seen this advice time and again, with the caveat that your egg will crack if you don't. This is one of those myths that come from a germ of truth. Years ago, before factory farms and cold storage, eggs were seasonal. Come winter, eggs were dear. A farmer would store eggs and sell them in February, when the price would be high. The farmer used something called water glass to preserve eggs. Water glass is the chemical sodium silicate. When mixed with water it forms a protective gel, which sealed off the pores of the eggshell. So if you boiled an egg that had been preserved in such a way, the air in the egg would have caused the shell to explode—unless you had pricked the end with a needle.

If your eggs crack when hard-cooking, it is likely that the shells were thin. Older chickens lay thin-shelled, fragile eggs, even when fed oyster shell for calcium. That's yet another reason why commercial farms don't keep chickens past the second molt (at 28 months of age). Egg breakage is too costly. I've learned to put thin-shelled eggs gently in the egg basket and to not hard-cook them. But any way you cook eggs, the fresh ones from your own hens are more delicious than any you can get in the supermarket.

Hard-Cooked Eggs: Two Methods

Is a recipe for hard-cooked eggs necessary? Yes! If you've ever had a tough egg that you were tempted to bounce instead of eat, or found an egg with a green yolk, then these directions are for you. Most people boil eggs, but that high heat causes the whites to harden up to a rubbery texture. Also, that unsavory-looking green tinge around the yolk is due to a reaction of the iron and sulfur in the egg yolks that only occurs at high heat. So instead of boiling, use one of the methods here.

Hot Water Immersion Method for Hard-Cooked Eggs

1. Place the eggs in a pot and cover with 2 inches of water. Bring the water to a simmer. Don't let the water come to a rolling boil. As soon as the water is simmering, cover the pot and remove from the heat. Set a timer for 12 minutes for small, 16 minutes for large, and 18 minutes for jumbo eggs.

2. Meanwhile, fill a bowl with ice water.

3. When the timer goes off, drain the water out of the pot. Immediately immerse the eggs in the ice water.

4. When the eggs are cold to the touch, remove them from the water and peel. Do this by rolling them to crackle the shells. Or, shake the bowl to crackle all of the shells. Store, peeled or still in the shell, in a covered container in the refrigerator for up to 4 days for optimum quality.

Steaming Method for Hard-Cooked Eggs

You can buy adorable egg steamers that look like chickens, and vintage steamers made of porcelain, but I use a pot with a steamer basket in it. For large quantities of eggs, I use my wok and the steamer basket. This method works best when the eggs are in one layer and not piled on top of each other.

1. Put a steamer basket into a pot filled with water to reach the underside of the steamer. Set the eggs in the basket and cover.

2. Bring to a boil, then reduce to a simmer. Set a timer for 20 minutes.

3. Meanwhile, fill a bowl with ice water.

4. When the timer goes off, immediately remove the eggs and immerse in the ice water. When the eggs are cold to the touch, remove them from the water and peel. Do this by rolling them to crackle the shells. Or, shake the bowl to crackle all of the shells. Store in a covered container in the refrigerator for up to 4 days for optimum quality.

Soft-Cooked Eggs

There is something indulgent about eating a soft-cooked or coddled egg right out of the shell. It has to do with the silky texture of the white balanced against the barely oozing, rich yolk. Serve in a beautiful eggcup with a dusting of seasoned salt (page 79), and your basic egg is transformed. Cut toast into long strips, often poetically called "soldiers," to dip into the yolk.

Makes 4 eggs

4 large eggs

1.   Bring a small pot of water to a boil. Add the eggs and immediately cover and remove the pot from the burner.

2.   Let the eggs sit in the hot water for 3 to 4 minutes. Using tongs or a slotted spoon, remove each egg and place it in an eggcup.

3.   Take a knife or spoon and tap along the top of the egg to break the shell and remove the top of the egg. There are tools made for this purpose that will make a clean slice, but I think that a ragged edge looks attractively rustic. Use a spoon to eat the egg right out of the shell. Small eggs will require tiny spoons. I prefer to coddle the largest eggs, and set aside the extra-large eggs from my Delaware hen, Opal, for this purpose.

Tea Eggs

Tea eggs are hard-cooked eggs that are steeped in tea infused with Asian spices. After a long marinade, the shelled eggs take on the look of marble. If I have a party coming up, I save the eggs from my bantam hens to make tea eggs. These small eggs are the right size to serve as finger food. Put them on a platter with a bowl of Szechuan Pepper Salt (recipe follows) for dipping. Tea eggs are also very good on a bed of sesame noodles.

Makes 6 eggs

6 large eggs

4 cups water

4 bags orange pekoe tea or black tea

1 tablespoon soy sauce

1 tablespoon kosher salt

2 star anise

1 large slice fresh ginger

1. Hard-cook the eggs according to one of the methods on page 75.

2. While the eggs are in the ice bath, boil the 4 cups water and place the tea bags, soy sauce, salt, star anise, and ginger in a heat-proof bowl. Pour in the boiling water and stir.

3. Remove the eggs from the ice water. Gently crack the shells all over but do not peel. Put the eggs into the tea bath. Cover and refrigerate for at least 24 or up to 48 hours. Discard the liquids and peel the eggs.

Seasoned Salts

Hard-cooked eggs and salt are made for each other. When served with a selection of seasoned salts, hard-cooked eggs become special enough for a party. I also like to have seasoned salts on hand for everyday cooking. Put a touch in scrambled eggs, dust some on fish, or try the Szechuan Pepper Salt with some stir-fried vegetables. Seasoned salts are the essence of farmstead cooking—a few simple ingredients of excellent quality prepared with care but not fuss. Stored in airtight jars out of direct sunlight, these salts will stay fresh for several months.

Each of these recipes makes ½ cup of seasoned salt

½ cup kosher salt

1 teaspoon white peppercorns

2 tablespoons pink peppercorns

1 tablespoon green peppercorns

Three-Pepper Salt

1. Put all of the ingredients into a medium sauté pan and place over medium heat. Toss and toast until the salt begins to color. Transfer to a bowl and let cool.

2. Grind in a spice mill or food processor until finely ground. Store in a glass jar.

½ cup kosher salt

1 tablespoon dried lemon zest

2 teaspoons dried orange zest

1 teaspoon dried thyme

1 teaspoon celery seeds

1 teaspoon paprika

Citrus Salt

If you don't dry your own citrus peels, dried orange and lemon zest can be found in jars in the spice section of the supermarket.

Grind all of the ingredients in a spice mill or food processor until finely ground. Store in a glass jar.

½ cup kosher salt

¼ cup Szechuan peppercorns

2 teaspoons coriander seeds

1 tablespoon Chinese five-spice powder

Szechuan Pepper Salt

1. Heat a dry, heavy skillet over medium heat. Add the salt, peppercorns, and coriander seeds. Toast until fragrant but not browned, about 3 minutes. Shake the pan as they toast. Stir in the five-spice powder. Transfer to a bowl and let cool.

2. Grind in a spice mill or food processor until finely ground. Sift through a fine-mesh sieve to remove the coarse bits of peppercorn husks. Store in a glass jar.

Pickled Beets and Eggs

Eggs don't get any prettier than this. The whites absorb the beet juice and turn purple, and yet the yolks remain bright yellow. Not only are these beautiful, but they taste great, too. Add pickled eggs to a green salad, use them in the Cobb Salad (page 88), or serve them quartered with the beets as part of an antipasto plate.

Makes 6 to 12 servings

6 to 12 large eggs, hard-cooked and peeled

8 small beets, cooked, peeled, and quartered, or one 15-ounce can whole beets, drained

1½ cups apple cider vinegar

1½ cups water

2 teaspoons kosher salt

2 tablespoons granulated sugar

1 teaspoon yellow mustard seeds

½ red onion, sliced

1. Place the eggs and beets in a glass container or jar with a tight-fitting lid.

2. Place all of the remaining ingredients in a small saucepan and bring to a boil for 3 minutes. Remove from the heat and let cool to lukewarm.

3. Pour the contents of the pot over the eggs and beets. Refrigerate for at least 1 day. Eat within 2 weeks.

HARD-COOKED EGG TIPS

Deviled eggs and other recipes that call for showing off the yolks are best prepared with eggs that have the yolks in the center. It's so frustrating to slice an egg in half and find that one wall of whites is as thin as paper. An egg is designed by nature to have the yolk in the center, which is essential for a chick to grow inside. There are two stringy cords, the chalazae, that hold the yolk in place. As the egg ages, these break down, allowing the yolk to shift and press against the shell. *To keep the yolk centered, always store eggs pointy end down.*

Also, have you ever noticed that some eggs have large air pockets and when hard-cooked, the eggs look flat on one side? That's because there are two membranes surrounding the whites—an outer one is next to the shell, and an inner membrane holds the egg whites together. When an egg is just laid, those membranes are stuck together, but as the egg ages and air seeps into the egg through its pores, the two separate. During storage, water in the egg evaporates, and this air cell becomes increasingly larger. So, although older eggs are easier to peel, if they are too old they will have flattened sides from air pockets.

Although eggs remain delicious for hard-cooking up to 3 weeks after laying, for these reasons *I try to use eggs about 10 days old for recipes that require pretty eggs with the yolks in the center.* Every day, after collecting the eggs, I put them into a cardboard carton (friends give me their used supermarket containers), and *I write the date on the lid and put the eggs right into the refrigerator. I know which eggs are best for frying (the freshest!) and which are best for hard-cooking. Older eggs go into baked goods.* All will be used, that's for sure.

Eggs and Croutons for Steamed Vegetables

Vegetables topped with this mixture become special enough to be served as a first course or a summer lunch. You can prepare the separate components ahead of time, and then compose a platter of steamed vegetables and the egg topping right before serving, which makes this a convenient choice for a relaxed brunch party.

Makes 6 servings

2 slices bread, cut into tiny cubes
   no larger than ¼ inch

1 lemon

½ teaspoon salt

⅛ teaspoon freshly ground
   black pepper

¼ cup chopped fresh parsley

5 tablespoons extra-virgin olive oil

3 large eggs, hard-cooked
   and minced

3 to 4 cups steamed vegetables of
   your choice (chilled or warm)

1. Preheat the oven to 350°F. Put the bread cubes on a baking sheet in a single layer. Bake for 5 to 10 minutes, until dried out but not browned.

2. Zest the lemon using a Microplane grater (or other tool of your choice). You need about 1 tablespoon zest. Juice the lemon. One lemon should yield about ¼ cup juice, strained.

3. Place the salt, pepper, parsley, and zest in a small bowl and set aside.

4. Warm 3 tablespoons of the oil in a large skillet. Add the bread cubes and toss so that all sides are coated with oil. Cook until toasty and crunchy, which will be a matter of only a few minutes. Transfer to a bowl.

5. Toss the seasoning in with the bread cubes. Stir in the minced eggs.

6. Whisk together the lemon juice and remaining 2 tablespoons olive oil. Pour over the vegetables in a bowl, using only as much of this dressing as necessary to coat the vegetables. Reserve extra for another use.

7. Place the vegetables on a serving plate and top with the egg and crouton mixture.

Classic Deviled Eggs

Deviled eggs can by stylish or kitschy. They suit any event, from a picnic to an elegant cocktail party. This is the basic version, but if made with farmstead eggs, with their bright yellow and flavorful yolks, they become something truly special. Creativity is encouraged! Keep these classic, or dress them up with crème fraîche, goat cheese, caviar, chutney, or smoked salmon. It's hard to go wrong with deviled eggs.

Makes 12 egg halves

6 large eggs, hard-cooked and peeled

2 tablespoons mayonnaise

½ teaspoon Dijon mustard

¼ teaspoon dry mustard (such as Colman's)

¼ teaspoon kosher salt

⅛ teaspoon freshly ground black pepper

1½ teaspoons sweet pickle relish

Sweet paprika, for garnish

1. Slice the eggs in half lengthwise. Remove the yolks and put them in a small bowl.

2. Using a fork, mash the mayonnaise, mustards, salt, and pepper with the egg yolks. Combine until smooth. Stir in the relish until it is evenly distributed.

3. Put the filling in a plastic sandwich bag. Cut off a corner and squeeze the filling into the egg whites. If desired, use a pastry bag with a decorative tip. Dust with paprika.

Curried Shrimp Deviled Eggs

Wild-caught shrimp have better flavor and are a more environmentally sound choice than farm-raised shrimp. Or, use shredded crabmeat as an alternative to the shrimp.

Makes 12 egg halves

6 large eggs, hard-cooked
   and peeled

2 tablespoons mayonnaise

½ teaspoon kosher salt

¼ teaspoon Asian chili paste

1½ teaspoons lime juice

2 teaspoons chopped fresh cilantro

½ teaspoon ground cumin

½ teaspoon curry powder

16 small shrimp, cooked and shelled

Fresh cilantro leaves, for garnish
   (optional)

1. Slice the eggs in half lengthwise. Remove the yolks and put them in a small bowl.

2. Using a fork, mash the egg yolks with the mayonnaise, salt, chili paste, lime juice, chopped cilantro, cumin, and curry powder until smooth.

3. Finely mince 4 of the shrimp and stir into the yolk mixture.

4. Put the filling in a plastic sandwich bag. Cut off a corner and squeeze the mixture into the egg whites. Top each egg with a shrimp. If desired, garnish each with a cilantro leaf.

Egg Salad with Chives

Use this recipe as a guide, but feel free to improvise. For a garden club potluck I picked tarragon, chives, basil, and bronze fennel from my garden, finely minced these herbs, and mashed them with the eggs and a touch of mayonnaise. People loved it and asked, "What's in here?" The answer was easy: a few fresh herbs and very good eggs. Pickle relish is also good when mixed into egg salad—especially if the relish was bought at a farm stand.

Makes enough filling for 2 sandwiches

4 large eggs, hard-cooked, peeled, and quartered

¼ cup mayonnaise

2 tablespoons minced celery

1 tablespoon minced fresh chives

1 tablespoon minced fresh parsley

⅛ teaspoon kosher salt

⅛ teaspoon freshly ground black pepper

1. Mash the eggs and mayonnaise together with a fork until the mixture is the desired consistency. I like it uneven and chunky. If you want it tidy and smooth, start with thinly sliced eggs.

2. Add all of the remaining ingredients and stir with a fork until combined.

Egg, Potato, and Tuna Salad

This sturdy salad is good as a main course at home, or take it to work for a brown bag lunch. Although waxy potatoes, such as Yukon golds, hold together well in salads, leftover baked russets can be used in a pinch. This is a recipe to get creative with; steamed broccoli and asparagus are good add-ins. In the springtime, when my garden overflows with spinach, I'll add a large handful. Water-packed solid albacore tuna is acceptable here, although oil-packed tuna has more flavor. Canned salmon is also a good option. It's your choice.

Makes 4 servings

8 ounces small new potatoes (red or white)

4 large eggs, hard-cooked, peeled, and quartered

One 6-ounce can tuna, drained

1 rib celery, chopped

¼ cup chopped red onion or scallion

1 tablespoon chopped fresh parsley

1 tablespoon minced fresh dill

1 teaspoon grated lemon zest

½ teaspoon kosher salt

¼ teaspoon freshly ground black pepper

FOR THE DRESSING:

1 tablespoon mayonnaise

1 tablespoon lemon juice

1 tablespoon extra-virgin olive oil

1 tablespoon coarse mustard

1 teaspoon granulated sugar

1. Bring a medium pot of water to a boil and boil the potatoes until just tender. Let cool, and then cut into quarters.

2. Put the potatoes and eggs in a bowl. Flake the tuna and add to the bowl. Gently mix these ingredients. Add the celery, onion, parsley, dill, and lemon zest and toss gently. Add the salt and pepper, and stir once more.

3. Whisk the dressing ingredients together until well blended. Pour over the salad and toss to coat.

Dinosaur Kale and Egg Panzanella Salad

Dinosaur kale has an elongated and flatter leaf than regular kale. It is also sweeter and is delicious raw. If unavailable, don't substitute curly kale, but instead make this with romaine lettuce.

Use a sturdy, crusty bread here. Really good imported Parmigiano-Reggiano cheese is pricey. Unfortunately, the less expensive versions don't have enough flavor for this salad. If you can't get the real cheese, use something else. When I'd rather not splurge on the best Parmesan, I substitute a tangy sheep's milk feta.

Makes 6 servings

2 cups cubed bread

½ cup coarsely chopped walnuts

2 cups dinosaur kale cut into chiffonade

2 cups cubed tomatoes or halved cherry tomatoes

⅓ cup grated Parmesan cheese

⅓ cup lemon juice (from 2 large lemons)

3 tablespoons olive oil

½ teaspoon kosher salt

¼ teaspoon freshly ground black pepper

2 large eggs, hard-cooked, peeled, and quartered

1. Preheat the oven to 350°F. Toast the bread and walnuts on a baking sheet for about 7 minutes. Let cool.

2. In a large bowl, toss the kale, tomatoes, and cheese together. Stir in the bread and nuts.

3. Whisk together the lemon juice, oil, salt, and pepper. Pour over the salad and toss to coat. Top with the eggs.

Cobb Salad

You can't go wrong with this classic if you use the best ingredients. If perfectly ripe tomatoes aren't available, then leave them out. Use whatever greens look fresh and crisp. Romaine mixed with mesclun or Bibb and green leaf are well suited to this salad. Get the best slab bacon available. Even selecting a good-quality red wine vinegar will make a difference.

Makes 4 servings

FOR THE DRESSING:

2 tablespoons red wine vinegar

4 tablespoons extra-virgin olive oil

¼ teaspoon kosher salt

¼ teaspoon freshly ground black pepper

½ teaspoon granulated sugar

1 teaspoon Dijon mustard

FOR THE SALAD:

4 cups mixed salad greens (about 8 ounces)

¼ cup chopped mixed fresh herbs (basil, parsley, mint, and chives are good options)

4 slices bacon, cooked until crisp and drained

1 ripe avocado, pitted, peeled, and sliced

4 large eggs, hard-cooked, peeled, and quartered

¼ cup crumbled blue cheese

2 cups sliced deli turkey cut into long strips

2 medium tomatoes, sliced

1. In a small bowl, whisk together the dressing ingredients.

2. In a large bowl, toss the greens with the fresh herbs. Toss with 2 tablespoons of the dressing. Place the greens on a platter or in a large, shallow serving bowl.

3. Arrange the rest of the ingredients on top of the greens. Use your creativity. A starburst pattern is attractive in a bowl. Or use a rectangular serving platter and arrange the ingredients in alternating strips, making sure that the colors and textures are balanced.

4. Sprinkle the remaining dressing over the top.

Salmon and Egg Pan Bagnat

Pan bagnat, a sandwich from Nice, France, means "bathed bread," which comes from the moisture of the oils and flavors of the ingredients soaking into the bread. It is often better the second day. Tuna is the usual filling, but I like salmon, too, and use it in this version. The other ingredients can be tweaked as well. In the winter, when ripe tomatoes and fresh basil are hard to find, use pesto and roasted red peppers. But always use good eggs! The rich yolks are a soothing counterpoint to the briny olives and the assertive flavor of the salmon.

Any bread that is crusty and rustic will make a good pan bagnat. Regular sandwich bread won't do because the pan bagnat will become soggy and fall apart. Sometimes it is made with a baguette, but I prefer a wider loaf such as an Italian ciabatta.

Makes 4 servings

FOR THE DRESSING:

3 tablespoons extra-virgin olive oil

1 tablespoon mayonnaise

1 tablespoon lemon juice

2 teaspoons red wine vinegar

¼ teaspoon kosher salt

⅛ teaspoon freshly ground
  black pepper

FOR THE SANDWICH:

One 1-pound loaf crusty bread

One 5-ounce can salmon, drained

1 tablespoon drained capers

¼ cup pitted and sliced kalamata
  or Niçoise olives

1 tablespoon minced fresh chives,
  red onion, or scallion

2 tablespoons minced fresh parsley

4 large eggs, hard-cooked, peeled,
  and sliced

2 radishes, thinly sliced

6 large basil leaves

½ medium tomato, sliced

1. Whisk all of the dressing ingredients together in a bowl.

2. Cut the bread loaf in half lengthwise and brush some of the dressing on each cut side of the bread.

3. With a fork, combine the remaining dressing with the salmon, capers, and olives. Spread the mixture onto the bread.

4. Distribute the chives and parsley on the mixture. Top with the eggs, radishes, basil, tomato, and the other half of the bread.

5. Slice the loaf into quarters. Wrap each tightly with plastic wrap and then with aluminum foil. Refrigerate, and eat within 24 hours.

Beef and Egg Piroshki

This is a meat pie with a typical Polish filling, and so I am calling it a "piroshki," but similar savory turnovers are seen in many other cultures, from Wales to Mexico. What sets this one apart and gives it an Eastern European flavor is the hard-cooked egg and fresh dill. If you can find frozen puff pastry that lists butter as the only fat, buy that, as it is higher quality than other kinds. I've found that it's best to defrost it in the refrigerator for several hours. If defrosted on the counter, some of the dough goes a tad soggy before the center defrosts.

Makes 10 to 12 meat pies

1 tablespoon vegetable oil

¾ cup minced onion (from 1 medium)

8 ounces ground beef

¼ teaspoon kosher salt

¼ teaspoon freshly ground black pepper

2 teaspoons minced fresh dill or 1 tablespoon chopped fresh parsley

3 large eggs, hard-cooked, peeled, and minced

1 package puff pastry (14 to 16 ounces), thawed

1 large egg, beaten with 2 tablespoons water

1. Preheat the oven to 375°F.

2. Heat the oil in a medium skillet over medium heat. Sauté the onion in the oil until the onion softens. Add the beef and stir and cook until browned. Transfer to a bowl and stir in the salt, pepper, and dill until well mixed. Gently stir in the eggs.

3. Flour a work surface and roll out the puff pastry until ⅛ inch thick. Cut out 4-inch circles using a biscuit cutter, or trace around a bowl with a sharp paring knife (that's what I do).

4. Put a heaping tablespoon on half of a circle. Fold over and seal by pressing with the tines of a fork. Place on a baking sheet. Repeat until all of the dough is used, to make 10 to 12 piroshkies. There might be some meat mixture left over.

5. Brush the pies with the beaten egg. Put the baking sheet in the oven and bake for 25 to 30 minutes, until browned and puffy. These make excellent leftovers. You can also make smaller pies to serve as party finger food.

Poached and Shirred Eggs

Poached and shirred eggs are eggs that, although they're cooked without their shells, are kept whole, soft, and pliable. Poached eggs are gently set into simmering water. The heat immediately firms up the white so that the egg stays together. Poached eggs can be cooked until set all the way through or done so quickly that the yolks remain runny. You'll often see directions for poached eggs that look quite fussy. That's because supermarket eggs are thin and fragile. One trick to keeping eggs whole as they poach is to add a touch of vinegar to the water. This makes the protein in the egg whites congeal. I include that instruction in the directions on the following page. But fresh farmstead eggs have intact membranes that keep them together, sturdy yolks that don't break, and thick whites that don't disperse into strands in the water, and they usually don't require the addition of vinegar. I prefer to poach eggs simply in salted water—to do that I use eggs that were laid within hours of cooking.

Shirred eggs are similar to poached but are baked uncovered in a buttered dish, usually with a little cream or other liquid to add interest. You don't have to be as careful with shirred eggs, because they are baked in cups. Still, a fresh farmstead egg, with a dark yellow-orange dome of a yolk, is the prettiest and yummiest shirred egg to be had.

A hybrid between poached and shirred are eggs that are "poached" in a cup. You can purchase silicone poaching cups that float on simmering water. I have a couple; I coat them generously with olive oil and crack in the eggs. There are also vintage cups to be found that require a good greasing and that sit in a shallow, covered pan of simmering water. I have one that is shaped like a daisy: The yolk is the center and the whites spread out to become the petals. So pretty!

Poached Eggs

Poached eggs are soft, free-form egg packets. Rarely made at home, they are most often seen on restaurant brunch menus in eggs Benedict. This is too bad, because poached eggs are easy to prepare and can be used in any number of ways. My favorite weekday breakfast is a poached egg served in half an avocado.

These directions are for poaching 4 eggs at a time. You can poach several batches of eggs in the same liquid until it becomes cloudy from strands of egg white. Poached eggs can be made a day in advance. To store, place the eggs in a bowl of cold water and keep refrigerated until you are ready to reheat them. To reheat, slip the eggs into water that is hot but not simmering (150°F) and let them warm through. They can also be held in this hot water bath for 30 minutes before serving.

Makes 4 eggs

2 teaspoons white wine vinegar

1 teaspoon kosher salt

4 large eggs

1. Fill a saucepan with water 3 inches deep. Add the vinegar and salt. Bring to a simmer. Lower the temperature so that the water is just moving.

2. Fill a small bowl with cold water. Crack an egg into another small bowl. Slip the egg into the hot water. If the egg sticks to the bottom, gently release it with a spatula. Add each egg in this way. Do not crowd. As the eggs cook, the whites will solidify. Don't worry if they look messy with strands. Poach for 3 minutes for a soft-cooked egg with a runny yolk or up to 6 minutes for a firm yolk. Once the eggs are set to your liking, use a slotted spoon to remove them. Dip each egg into the bowl of cold water. This will rinse off the vinegar and stop the cooking.

3. If desired, take kitchen scissors and trim the ragged egg whites.

Asparagus with Poached Eggs and Smoked Salmon

Most of my hens are "standard," which means they are big girls, weighing 4 to 6 pounds each. A hen of that size lays an egg that weighs about 2 ounces, which is what the USDA calls "large." But I also like to keep a bantam or two. These hens are half the size of their large companions, and their eggs are smaller, too. For this recipe, if I have them, I'll use two bantam eggs instead of one large egg for a charming presentation.

Makes 4 servings

FOR THE DRESSING:

2 tablespoons lemon juice

2 tablespoons mayonnaise

⅓ cup vegetable or olive oil

1 tablespoon whole-grain mustard

1 teaspoon granulated sugar

1 teaspoon minced fresh dill

¼ teaspoon kosher salt

⅛ teaspoon freshly ground black pepper

FOR THE ASSEMBLED DISH:

12 asparagus spears

4 slices bread of your choice

8 ounces smoked salmon

4 large eggs, poached and kept warm

Chopped fresh dill, for garnish

1. Whisk all of the dressing ingredients together.

2. Set up a steamer basket and steam the asparagus spears just until tender. When the asparagus is done, toast the bread.

3. Assemble this recipe on individual dinner plates. Put a piece of toast on each plate. Arrange the salmon and asparagus on each piece of toast. Top each with an egg. Drizzle the dressing over the egg and asparagus. Garnish with dill.

Green Salad with Bacon and Poached Eggs

The combination of seemingly disparate ingredients of salty bacon, crunchy croutons, silky and oozing poached eggs, and bright greens is pulled together into a complex and yet cohesive whole by the mustard vinaigrette. Onions, when used raw in a salad, can overwhelm the other ingredients. But shallots are a mild and sophisticated member of the onion family and, when finely minced and added to a dressing, supply just the right amount of sharpness without being overpowering. Shallot bulbs vary greatly in size, which is why I provide a volume measurement. All shallots, whether the size of a clove, a cherry tomato, or a pearl onion, should have the same mellow flavor.

Makes 4 servings

2 cups bread cubes

2 tablespoons olive oil

6 cups mixed salad greens

4 slices bacon, cooked until crispy
   and chopped

4 large eggs

FOR THE DRESSING:

3 tablespoons red wine vinegar

1 teaspoon Dijon mustard

1 teaspoon granulated sugar

2 tablespoons extra-virgin olive oil

2 tablespoons finely minced shallots

¼ teaspoon kosher salt

1. There are some excellent brands of croutons in the market, but to make your own, preheat the oven to 400°F. Toss the bread cubes with the olive oil. Spread out in a single layer on a baking sheet and toast in the oven for 4 minutes, then turn over and bake for another 4 to 5 minutes, until lightly browned. Allow the croutons to cool.

2. Toss the greens, croutons, and bacon in a large salad bowl.

3. Poach the eggs (page 93).

4. Meanwhile, whisk together the dressing ingredients and pour over the salad. Toss to coat.

5. Arrange the salad on plates and immediately top each portion with a hot poached egg.

Poached Eggs in Twice-Baked Potatoes

This is great for a brunch crowd because it can be assembled a day ahead and baked just before the company arrives. For a party, select potatoes that have the same medium size and shape so that they all finish cooking at the same time. Make portions modest so that your guests have room for drinks and dessert!

Makes 2 servings

1 large baking potato (about 12 ounces), scrubbed clean

¼ cup shredded cheddar or Monterey Jack cheese

2 tablespoons sour cream

2 teaspoons unsalted butter, softened

1 slice bacon, cooked until crisp and drained

¼ teaspoon kosher salt

⅛ teaspoon freshly ground black pepper

2 large eggs

1 tablespoon grated Parmesan cheese

1 tablespoon sliced fresh chives or scallions (optional)

1. Preheat the oven to 375°F. Scrub the potato until it is very clean, and bake the potato until a knife can be easily inserted in the center. Allow the potato to cool so it can be handled. Leave the oven on.

2. Cut the potato in half lengthwise. If necessary, cut off a small slice from the bottom of each half so that the potatoes sit flat. Scoop out the potato to within ¼ inch from the skin. (A serrated grapefruit knife makes easy work of this task.) Set aside ¼ cup of the potato for this recipe, reserving any remaining potato for another use.

3. Combine the potato flesh, cheddar cheese, sour cream, and butter. Mash until mostly smooth. Crumble in the bacon and stir until it is evenly distributed. Stir in the salt and pepper.

4. Mound the filling in each potato half. Make an indentation in the center for the egg. Place the potatoes in a baking dish.

5. Poach the eggs for 1 minute (page 93) so that the white is set but the yolk remains runny. Put a poached egg in the hollow of each potato half. Sprinkle the Parmesan on top.

6. Bake for 10 minutes, or until the cheese begins to brown. Garnish with the chives.

Eggs Poached in Marinara

I rely on this dish on the nights when I think there is nothing in the house and I don't want to cook. I always have eggs and cheese in the fridge, sausage in the freezer, and a jar of tomato sauce in the pantry. Serve this with crusty bread, polenta, or pasta.

Makes 4 servings

6 to 8 ounces sausage of your choice

2½ cups marinara sauce (or one 24-ounce jar)

4 large eggs

Parmesan cheese, for serving

1. Brown the sausage in a medium saucepan over medium heat. If there is excess fat, drain it off.

2. Lower the heat and pour the tomato sauce into the pan. Bring to a gentle simmer. Heat until the sausage is fully cooked.

3. Carefully crack the eggs into the sauce, so that they remain whole and are not touching. Cover the pot and cook for 6 to 8 minutes, until the egg yolks have just firmed up.

4. Ladle onto crusty toast, polenta, or pasta, with a piece of sausage and an egg for each diner. Generously grate the cheese on top.

Italian Egg Soup

Although reminiscent of the classic Italian soup *stracciatella,* you won't find my recipe in an Italian cookbook. It's something I came up with that uses Italian ingredients in a way that satisfies me. This soup is thick, deeply flavorful, and easy to prepare, and it uses ingredients that I always have on hand.

Makes 6 servings

6 ounces baby spinach

3 tablespoons extra-virgin olive oil

½ cup cubed pancetta

1 cup chopped onion

2 cloves garlic, minced

⅓ cup arborio rice

6 cups chicken broth

¼ cup grated Romano cheese

4 large eggs

Kosher salt

Freshly ground black pepper

Crushed hot red pepper flakes

1. Wash the spinach (even if the bag says "washed"). Discard any mushy leaves. Heat the olive oil in a large pot. Toss in the pancetta and onion, and cook until the pancetta begins to brown and crisp and the onion softens and turns golden. Add the garlic and cook for a few minutes more.

2. Add the spinach to the pot and cook for about 2 minutes, until wilted. Stir in the rice.

3. Pour in the broth and bring to a simmer. Cover and cook at a low simmer for 20 minutes.

4. Using a fork, stir the cheese and eggs together in a bowl until well combined. Take the pot off the heat and, if desired, pour the soup into a serving tureen. Immediately stir in the egg-cheese mixture. It will cook when it hits the hot soup. Taste and season with salt and pepper if necessary (this will depend on the saltiness of the broth). Sprinkle with hot red pepper flakes.

Spanish Garlic Soup

This soup has the big flavors and full body that are perfect for a winter dinner. It is finished in the oven like French onion soup, but in this case, instead of melted cheese, there is an egg poached on the surface.

Makes 4 servings

3 tablespoons olive oil

6 cloves garlic, sliced

1 teaspoon sweet paprika

½ teaspoon ground cumin

⅛ teaspoon ground saffron

4 thick slices crusty French bread

4 cups chicken broth

½ to 1 teaspoon kosher salt

Freshly ground black pepper

4 large eggs

2 tablespoons chopped fresh cilantro or parsley

1. Heat the olive oil in a large pot. Add the garlic and cook over low heat for about 10 minutes, until the garlic is soft and golden. Take care not to let it scorch or turn dark brown. Properly cooked, garlic becomes sweet and pungent but loses its sharpness.

2. Stir in the paprika, cumin, and saffron. Heat for 1 minute, until the aromas intensify.

3. Place the bread in the seasoned oil and toast on both sides.

4. Pour the broth in carefully over the bread. Season with the salt and pepper. Bring the broth to a boil and then immediately lower the heat to a low simmer. If the soup boils too rapidly, the bread will break apart. That won't ruin it, but it looks much nicer with whole slices. Simmer for 20 minutes. Taste and add more salt if necessary (the saltiness of broth varies).

5. Preheat the oven to 400°F. Put 4 ovenproof soup bowls on a baking sheet. Ladle the soup and a slice of bread into each bowl. Crack an egg into each soup bowl. Slide the baking sheet into the oven (it's much easier than handling each bowl) and bake until the yolks are set, 8 to 10 minutes. Sprinkle each serving with the cilantro.

EGGS IN SOUP

The poached eggs in Spanish Garlic Soup take on the flavor of the broth, and the runny yolks cut the intensity of the garlic. In other soup recipes the eggs are not kept whole, but they still have that poached egg silkiness. In all cases, when adding eggs to soup, stir them in during the last few minutes to prevent overcooking.

Egg Drop Soup

Restaurant versions of this soup are heavily thickened with cornstarch. This is a lighter, home-style recipe. It is very easy to prepare and makes a wonderful late-night supper when you come home tired and think there is nothing in the house. I try to keep homemade chicken broth in my freezer, but I also keep a good-quality product in my pantry. I look for brands that use the same ingredients that I would at home, which means no MSG, sugars, or stabilizers. I also prefer low-sodium versions, and salt to taste at the table.

Makes 4 servings

4 cups chicken broth

2 slices peeled fresh ginger
(about 1 by ⅛ inch)

2 cloves garlic, smashed and peeled

1 teaspoon kosher salt

2 large eggs

1 teaspoon dry sherry

2 scallions, sliced, using all the white
and most of the green

2 tablespoons chopped fresh cilantro

1. Bring the broth, ginger, and garlic to a boil in a large pot. Lower the heat and simmer gently for 5 minutes. Discard the ginger and garlic. Stir in the salt. Lower the heat to a very low simmer.

2. In a small bowl, mix the eggs and sherry with a fork. Pour the eggs into the soup in a slow, steady stream, swirling them into the soup. The eggs will set in strands.

3. Remove from the heat and stir in the scallions and cilantro. Serve immediately.

Avgolemono Soup

This Greek soup is lemony, salty, and frothy. It uses the most basic ingredients to create an addictive soup. But avgolemono soup will not work with insipid canned broth. If you don't have good homemade chicken broth, use the best prepared broth you can purchase. This Greek soup is lemony, salty, and frothy. It uses the most basic ingredients to create an addictive soup. Orzo is small, ovoid pasta. Cook it a little longer than you think necessary, as you want the center of the pasta to be cooked through until soft, not chewy. Although orzo is the classic pasta for this soup, any small shape will do, including alphabets, which are a perennial favorite in my family, even as my sons grow into teenagers.

Makes 6 servings

6 cups chicken broth

1 cup orzo or riso pasta

4 large eggs

¼ cup lemon juice

½ to 1 teaspoon kosher salt

Freshly ground black pepper

Minced fresh mint and/or sage, for garnish

1. Bring the broth to a simmer in a 3- to 4-quart saucepan. Add the orzo, cover, and simmer for 12 minutes. Take off the heat.

2. Using an electric handheld mixer, beat the eggs in a medium bowl until foamy. Add the lemon juice and continue to beat until frothy.

3. Once the orzo is cooked, scoop out 1 cup of the hot broth and add it to the egg mixture, beating as you pour it in. Then pour the egg and lemon froth mixture into the soup pot, beating continuously until foamy—it will resemble the texture of milk in a caffe latte.

4. Taste and add the salt and pepper if desired. Eat right away! Ladle into soup bowls and top with the fresh herbs. As this soup sits, it loses some of its ethereal quality, but leftovers will still taste good.

Shirred Eggs with Spinach and Cream

You have your choice of cheese here. Parmesan is a safe option, but this is a good opportunity to use up that little bit of interesting cheese that is languishing in the refrigerator.

This recipe serves one. If making these for a number of people, simply multiply the recipe as needed. Always bake in individual ramekins; the ramekins can be placed in a baking dish so that they are easy to handle going into and out of the oven. Shirred eggs can be assembled and then refrigerated for several hours before baking.

Makes 1 serving

1 teaspoon unsalted butter

2 tablespoons chopped spinach
(fresh or frozen)

1 tablespoon cream (heavy or light)

1 large egg

Kosher salt and freshly ground
black pepper

Ground nutmeg

1 tablespoon grated cheese of
your choice

1. Preheat the oven to 350°F.

2. Put the butter in a 6- to 8-ounce ovenproof ramekin. Melt it in the microwave (about 20 seconds) and swirl around to coat the bottom and sides.

3. Briefly cook the spinach until wilted, then squeeze out the excess liquid. (This can be done quickly in the microwave.) Put the spinach in the ramekin. Pour in the cream. Crack the egg into the ramekin. Sprinkle salt and pepper onto the egg. Dust with nutmeg. Top with the cheese.

4. Place the ramekin in the oven and bake for about 15 minutes, until the yolk begins to set. Serve hot.

Shirred Eggs on Polenta

Shirred eggs are usually very rich and made with cream. Not this version. Here the egg is baked on a bed of polenta and vegetables. Jarred bruschetta topping is available in large supermarkets as well as at gourmet stores and farm stands. There are many versions, some with a variety of vegetables and some with just tomatoes. With a jar on hand, this recipe takes less than a minute of preparation, but I've also supplied a recipe. Either way, serve with a thick slice of toast and a salad, and you have a hassle-free meal.

Makes 1 serving

½ teaspoon olive oil

One 1-inch-thick slice polenta (from a log of store-bought prepared polenta)

1½ tablespoons bruschetta topping (recipe follows, or use store-bought)

1 large egg

Kosher salt

Freshly ground black pepper

1 tablespoon grated Parmesan cheese

1. Preheat the oven to 350°F.

2. Swirl the olive oil in a 6-ounce ramekin to coat the bottom and sides.

3. Place the slice of polenta in the bottom of the ramekin. Spoon on the bruschetta topping. Crack the egg into the ramekin. Sprinkle salt and pepper over the egg. Sprinkle on the Parmesan.

4. Place the ramekin in the oven and bake for 15 minutes, or until the egg is set.

Bruschetta Topping

Makes 1½ cups

1 pound tomatoes

1 clove garlic, peeled

½ cup fresh basil

1½ teaspoons extra-virgin olive oil

¼ teaspoon dried or ½ teaspoon minced fresh oregano

½ teaspoon kosher salt

⅛ teaspoon freshly ground black pepper

⅛ teaspoon crushed red pepper flakes

1. Core the tomatoes and slice in half across their equators. Squeeze out and discard the seeds.

2. Finely mince the garlic by hand or in a food processor. Chop the tomatoes and basil either by hand or machine. Stir in all of the remaining ingredients.

Tip: Makes more than needed. Try leftovers as the base layer for a casserole of baked chicken thighs, or spread a thick fish steak with bruschetta topping before broiling.

Omelets and Frittatas

There are many ways to cook omelets. Short-order cooks spread a thin layer of eggs on the griddle and then fold them over and over to create a rectangle. When I worked the brunch service at a fancy café, we made overstuffed omelets in a skillet and at the last minute puffed them in the broiler. The French make a small omelet of only two or three eggs, cooked in a lot of butter. The eggs are shaken back and forth as they set, and then with a flick of the wrist they are folded over into a soft omelet. This "rolled technique" takes practice. I use a modified version in the recipes here.

It's important to whip the eggs with a whisk; don't just beat them with a fork. The whisking helps the omelet to stay soft and mound up as it cooks. Some recipes call for adding a touch of milk to the eggs, for flavor and moisture; some don't. I've seen many classic omelet recipes that call for water. However, farmstead eggs that have been laid within a day or two of cooking have yet to lose moisture and so don't need anything added at all.

Like an omelet, a frittata is a mixture of eggs and filling cooked in a skillet. But a frittata is not folded over; rather, it sets slowly in the pan and is often finished in the oven. It can handle many more eggs and heavier fillings than the classic French rolled omelet. Also, frittatas are so dense that they can be sliced into wedges and served at room temperature. I like to offer a selection of different frittatas at brunch. I make them before the guests arrive and display them on cake stands on my kitchen island. I'll also have a basket of breads and muffins, butter, cream cheese, jam, fruit compote, a green salad, and a sweet cobbler or a selection of home-baked cookies.

Omelet

[MASTER RECIPE]

Even if using a nonstick pan, you really do need to use a full tablespoon of butter. An omelet should cook gently in butter and easily slip out of the pan when done. A generous amount of good butter is the only ingredient that will impart the flavor and the consistency needed for a true omelet. If I want to prepare eggs without added fat, I poach or hard-cook them. But once in a while it's worth indulging in a classic omelet!

Makes 1 serving

2 large eggs

1 tablespoon unsalted butter

Salt and freshly ground black pepper

1. Whisk the eggs in a bowl until the volume increases a bit.

2. Heat a 10-inch nonstick omelet pan over medium-low heat. Melt the butter and swirl it around the pan.

3. Pour the eggs into the pan. As the eggs set, lift the edges with a plastic spatula, tilt the pan, and let the raw eggs run under the set ones. Continue to do this until the eggs are softly cooked and there is only a sheen of uncooked egg on the surface. Do not let the eggs brown.

4. Tilt the pan over the serving plate, and as the first third of the omelet settles on the plate, shake the pan and roll the rest of the omelet out so that it folds over itself.

Smoked Trout Omelet

This could be made with any other smoked fish. Trout is often the mildest choice, but salmon or even smoked bluefish would be good. Whichever fish you use, discard the skin and flake the flesh into bite-sized pieces—not too large, and not shredded into small bits. With a simple recipe like this, texture is all-important.

Makes 1 serving

2 large eggs

1 tablespoon milk

1 tablespoon unsalted butter

¼ cup shredded smoked trout

1 teaspoon minced fresh chives

1. Whisk the eggs and milk together in a bowl.

2. Heat a 10-inch nonstick omelet pan over medium-low heat. Melt the butter and swirl it around the pan.

3. Pour the eggs into the pan. As the eggs set, lift the edges with a plastic spatula, tilt the pan, and let the raw eggs run under the set ones. Continue to do this until most of the eggs are softly cooked and there is only a sheen of uncooked eggs on the surface. Do not let the eggs brown.

4. Distribute the trout and chives down the center of the omelet. Cover and cook for about 3 minutes, until the eggs are set.

5. Tilt the pan over the serving plate, and as the first third of the omelet settles on the plate, shake the pan and roll the rest of the omelet out so that it folds over itself.

Potato Frittata with Fresh Herbs

Cook up potatoes fresh for this recipe, or throw together a last-minute meal with leftover potatoes. The red potatoes specified here are waxy and hold together, but russets are fine if that's what you have on hand.

Makes 6 servings

8 ounces red potatoes

1 cup sliced red onion

1 teaspoon kosher salt

¼ teaspoon freshly ground black pepper

5 tablespoons olive oil

8 large eggs

1 tablespoon minced fresh parsley

½ teaspoon minced fresh rosemary

½ teaspoon minced fresh thyme

1. Preheat the oven to 425°F. Slice the potatoes ⅛ inch thick. Toss the potatoes, onion, salt, and pepper in a bowl with 2 tablespoons of the olive oil. Spread out in a single layer on a baking sheet and cook for 10 to 15 minutes, until browned. Stir once during baking. Remove from the oven and let cool. Lower the oven temperature to 400°F.

2. Whisk the eggs and fresh herbs together (you can use the same bowl you tossed the spuds in). Stir in the roasted potato mixture. Heat the remaining 3 tablespoons of olive oil in an ovenproof 10-inch skillet. (You can reduce that to 2 tablespoons if using a nonstick skillet.) Pour in the eggs. Cook over medium-low heat, covered, for 10 minutes. Slide a flexible heatproof spatula under the eggs every few minutes to keep the bottom from sticking.

3. When the eggs are almost totally set, uncover and put the skillet in the oven. Bake for a couple of minutes, until the top sets and is lightly browned. Remove from the oven carefully (the handle will be very hot!). Run the spatula under the eggs to loosen, and then slip the frittata onto a serving plate. Serve warm or at room temperature, cut into wedges.

Apple and Brie Omelet

This omelet requires a tart, firm apple. Granny Smith apples are suitable year-round, but when fall arrives and the local orchards have bushels of just-picked apples, all of which are crispy, juicy, and full of sharp apple flavor, I use those.

Makes 1 serving

1 tablespoon unsalted butter

1½ teaspoons light brown sugar

¼ tart, firm apple, peeled, cored, and thinly sliced

1 tablespoon raw pecans (whole or large pieces)

3 large eggs

1 tablespoon milk

1 ounce Brie cheese

1. In a 10-inch nonstick skillet, melt 1 teaspoon of the butter. Stir in the brown sugar. Sauté the apple slices until softened, then set aside, leaving as much of the butter and sugar in the pan as possible. Add the pecans to the pan and cook for a few minutes, until they begin to toast. Set aside. (If making multiples of this omelet, do this step for all the apples and nuts needed in one batch and then cook the individual omelets.)

2. Whisk the eggs and milk together in a bowl. Cut the cheese into cubes. You should have ¼ cup.

3. Melt the remaining 2 teaspoons butter in the pan. Pour in the eggs. Cook over low heat, lifting the setting edges of the eggs with a flexible spatula and letting the raw eggs run under the set ones. Continue to do this until it is almost entirely set but not browned.

4. Put the cheese cubes and apple slices on half of the omelet. Cover and cook over low heat for about 4 minutes, until the cheese has melted. Fold the omelet in half with the spatula and slip onto a dish. Top with the pecans.

Salsa and Guacamole Frittata

The colors and flavors of this frittata are happy and bright. Have fun selecting a salsa for this. A classic tomato salsa is excellent, but don't hesitate to use a fruit salsa, like apple or peach. Or, try a corn salsa. All will be good.

Makes 4 servings

1 tablespoon unsalted butter

6 large eggs

½ teaspoon kosher salt

3 tablespoons prepared guacamole

2 tablespoons salsa, drained if watery, plus more for serving (optional)

2 tablespoons canned black beans, rinsed and drained

3 tablespoons grated cheddar or Monterey Jack cheese or queso fresco

Sour cream, for serving (optional)

1. Preheat the oven to 425°F.

2. Place a 10-inch nonstick skillet or well-seasoned cast-iron pan over medium-low heat. Melt the butter.

3. Lightly mix the eggs and salt in a bowl. Pour into the heated skillet. Cover and cook for 5 minutes. Lift the egg with a spatula several times as it cooks and let the raw egg flow under the cooked egg so it gets closer to the heat.

4. When the eggs are halfway set, arrange teaspoonfuls of the guacamole and salsa on top of the frittata. Distribute the beans across the surface. Top with the cheese.

5. Cover and continue to cook gently for about 10 minutes more, until the eggs are almost entirely set.

6. Place the frittata, uncovered, in the oven and cook for 2 to 4 minutes, until the eggs set and puff and the cheese melts. Carefully remove the hot pan from the oven. Using a wide spatula, release the frittata from the pan and slip it onto a serving plate. If desired, serve with additional salsa and some sour cream on the side.

Zucchini and Mint Frittata

Mint is not just for iced tea and garnishes on plates! Used in a frittata, it adds just the right savory and herbal note to the vegetables. A frittata can be finished in the oven, or it can be flipped over in the pan and finished on the stove. This recipe gives directions for the stovetop version, but you can also finish it in a hot oven as in the previous frittata recipes.

Makes 6 servings

3 tablespoons olive oil

½ cup sliced onion

1 red bell pepper, julienned

1 pound zucchini, sliced

8 large eggs

¼ cup grated Parmesan cheese

¼ cup chopped fresh mint

½ teaspoon kosher salt

¼ teaspoon freshly ground
   black pepper

1. Heat 2 tablespoons of the olive oil in a 10-inch heavy skillet. Sauté the onion and bell pepper until soft and golden. Take your time on this step to fully develop the sweet flavors of these vegetables. Stir in the zucchini and continue to cook over low heat until the edges begin to brown. Set aside in a bowl.

2. In another bowl, whisk together the eggs, 3 tablespoons of the Parmesan, the mint, salt, and pepper.

3. Heat the remaining 1 tablespoon olive oil in the skillet. Pour in the eggs and then distribute the vegetables on top. Cover and cook over medium-low heat for about 15 minutes, until the eggs are set but not yet firm on top. Several times while the eggs are cooking, take a flexible spatula and run it along the edge and under the frittata to make sure the eggs are not sticking to the pan.

4. Take the skillet off the heat. Put a dinner plate over it and flip the frittata onto the plate. Then slip the frittata back into the pan, now with the bottom side up. Top with the remaining 1 tablespoon Parmesan. Cook for a few minutes more, until the eggs are fully cooked.

Gremolata-Ricotta Frittata

The bright flavors of gremolata—an Italian mixture of lemon zest, garlic, and parsley—give this frittata a spark. It can sometimes be tricky to use reduced-fat cheeses in baking, as recipes often turn out watery and bland-tasting. In this case however, I've found no difference when making this with low-fat ricotta cheese. I think that the spaghetti absorbs extra moisture and all of those good eggs provide flavor and perfect texture. So, use whole ricotta or, if you prefer, make it a tad lighter by using part-skim.

Makes 4 servings

¾ cup ricotta cheese

¼ cup grated Parmesan cheese

1 clove garlic, minced

3 tablespoons chopped fresh parsley

2 tablespoons chopped fresh basil

1 teaspoon grated lemon zest

½ teaspoon kosher salt

¼ teaspoon freshly ground
   black pepper

6 large eggs

2 cups cooked spaghetti

1 tablespoon olive oil

1. Preheat the oven to 425°F.

2. Using a fork, thoroughly combine the cheeses, garlic, parsley, basil, lemon zest, salt, and pepper in a medium bowl.

3. Stir in the eggs and continue to mix with a fork until well combined.

4. Toss in the pasta and stir until it is evenly coated with the egg mixture.

5. Heat the olive oil in a 10-inch ovenproof sauté pan. Pour in the egg mixture, cover, and cook over low heat for 15 minutes. Several times during cooking, slip a flexible spatula around the edges and partially under the frittata to keep it from sticking. After 10 to 15 minutes, the bottom will be light brown and all but the top should be set.

6. Put the frittata, uncovered, in the oven and bake until the top sets and begins to brown lightly, 4 to 6 minutes. Remove from the oven carefully (the handle will be very hot!) and slip onto a serving plate.

Cheesy Egg Puff with Greens Hash

This recipe makes eating fresh, nutritious greens easy and delicious. Use whatever looks good in the market—any green will do, such as kale, spinach, beet tops, or chard. The different greens do vary in flavor and texture. Some taste distinctly "green," and others taste mellower. Color varies, too. Be wary of rainbow chard; it is so pretty in the market, but the reds will dye the eggs pink. Also, some greens shrink considerably when cooked. You'll start with what looks like a massive amount of spinach, only to have a spare handful after sautéing. On the other hand, a few sturdy kale leaves will be all that you need. Don't let this put you off of greens! Have fun tasting and experimenting with the wide range out there. And, if you do have hens, you'll see that the girls love greens. You'll find yourself wanting to share the vegetables with your flock.

Makes 6 servings

Olive oil cooking spray

10 large eggs

1 cup milk

1½ teaspoons kosher salt

¼ teaspoon freshly ground
    black pepper

1½ cups grated cheese of your choice
    (5 ounces)

2 tablespoons olive oil

1 shallot, sliced (or ¼ cup diced
    red onion)

1 potato (about 8 ounces), diced

2 slices bacon, cooked and diced

1½ cups chopped greens

1. Preheat the oven to 450°F. Coat a 2-quart shallow casserole dish with olive oil cooking spray (or butter).

2. Whisk the eggs, milk, salt, and pepper together in a medium bowl until well mixed. Stir in the cheese. Pour into the casserole.

3. Bake for about 20 minutes, until set; the top will brown slightly and the center will spring back to the touch but not jiggle.

4. While the eggs are baking, heat the olive oil in a medium pan over medium heat and sauté the shallot until softened. Add the diced potato and cook until tender.

5. Add the bacon and greens to the pan and stir to wilt the greens. Cook over low heat until the eggs are ready.

6. Top the casserole with the greens hash and serve.

Savory Quiches, Tarts, and Stratas

Quiches, tarts, and stratas all start with beaten eggs, and often milk and cheese, and all are baked in the oven. Quiches are the most like pies and are, in fact, baked with a crust and in a pie plate. Tarts are not as tall, are often baked in a tart pan (shallow and with a removable bottom), and often have a distinct layer of ingredients arranged in the pan before the eggs are poured on top. Stratas are like a cross between a quiche and a bread pudding.

Quiche

The fat percentage of the milk you use for quiche is up to you; I've specified what I prefer. I've made quiche with 1 percent milk, which is fine, especially when the filling includes gooey cheese; in other recipes, it's better when at least half of the milk is whole milk. Looking for something decadent? Then use half milk and half cream. I find that heavy cream alone is too rich, though.

One cup of shredded cheese will provide flavor and hold it all together. The type of cheese is totally up to you. Use Brie, blue, Parmesan, cheddar, or whatever you happen to have. A bit of expensive leftover cheese, just starting to dry out, that you don't want to waste is the perfect reason to make a quiche.

Where you can get really creative is with the cup of add-ins. Vegetables and bits of meat or fish will all do. This should be a mixture of ingredients. (As delicious as bacon is, 1 cup would be too much!) Some vegetables can be added raw, while some require cooking. Those that you would normally eat crunchy, like red bell pepper and chives, are fine to add as is. But vegetables with a high water content, like spinach and zucchini, should be wilted and drained first. Some vegetables, like onions, require slow cooking to caramelize and sweeten them first.

Quiche is the ideal use for leftovers. Roasted vegetables are great add-ins, and all that I do is cut them into even dice before stirring them into the egg mixture. That bit of leftover roast chicken or baked salmon is just enough to make a meal when stirred into the egg mixture. Raw meats must be precooked before adding.

Finally, quiche requires salt and pepper. The intensity and saltiness of the cheese (and meat) will determine how much salt to add. However much you use, a good sea salt will bring out the best of the other ingredients. A touch of pepper (always freshly ground) will spark the flavors. Depending on the add-ins, you might also want to add fresh and dried herbs or spices.

Makes 8 servings

5 large eggs

1½ cups milk

1 cup shredded cheese of your choice

1 cup chopped add-ins, such as cooked vegetables, meat, and/ or poultry

Kosher salt and freshly ground black pepper

Dried or fresh herbs (optional)

1 prebaked 9-inch All-Purpose Pastry Crust (page 155)

1. Preheat the oven to 325°F.

2. Vigorously whisk the eggs and milk in a bowl for at least 1 minute, until well combined.

3. Stir in the cheese. Stir in the add-ins (if these are freshly sautéed vegetables, wait until they are at room temperature so that they don't curdle the eggs). Add salt, pepper, and dried herbs, if using.

4. Pour the mixture into the crust. If using fresh herbs, arrange on the surface.

5. Bake for 40 minutes or until the quiche is set and lightly browned.

Quiche with Bacon and Cheese

Slab bacon is thickly cut bacon that is usually not as sweet as regular breakfast bacon. It's especially good when the bacon is sourced from a local farmer and smokehouse. There is a huge difference in flavor and quality between supermarket bacon and small-batch bacon from pastured pigs. The latter is worth seeking out and splurging on.

Makes 6 servings

4 large eggs

1½ cups light cream or half-and-half

½ teaspoon kosher salt

1 cup grated sharp cheddar cheese

3 slices slab bacon, cooked, drained, and crumbled

1 prebaked 9-inch All-Purpose Pastry Crust (page 155)

1. Preheat the oven to 325°F.

2. Using an electric mixer, beat the eggs and cream for 1 minute, until the mixture increases slightly in volume. Stir in the salt, cheese, and bacon. Pour the mixture into the crust.

3. Bake for 35 to 40 minutes, until the center is just set and the edges begin to brown.

Onion Tart

Don't be fooled by the simple-sounding recipe title or the short list of ingredients. Magic happens when onions are cooked slowly in bacon fat. Even a basic, sharply flavored yellow onion becomes lusciously mellow after a long, slow cooking, but if you are able to find innately sweet onions at the market, like Vidalias, then this tart will have an incomparable, complex smoky and honeyed flavor.

Makes 8 servings

One 9-inch All-Purpose Pastry Crust (page 155)

4 slices thick-cut bacon

2 pounds onions, preferably sweet like Walla Walla or Vidalia, sliced (8 cups)

3 large eggs

¾ cup sour cream

¼ cup cream (heavy or light)

½ teaspoon kosher salt

1. Set the pastry dough into a 9-inch pie plate. Place in the freezer while cooking the bacon and onions.

2. Cook the bacon in a large, heavy sauté pan or cast-iron skillet over medium heat. Lift the bacon out, leaving the fat in the pan. Drain the bacon on paper towels, and then chop.

3. Cook the onions in the bacon grease over medium-low heat until they soften and turn a deep golden color. Don't rush this step. Let the sweet caramelized onion flavor slowly develop, which will take about 30 minutes. I usually cut onions by hand, but for this quantity I use a food processor.

4. Preheat the oven to 425°F.

5. In a bowl, whisk the eggs, sour cream, cream, and salt until smooth. Stir in the bacon.

6. Remove the pastry dough from the freezer and evenly spread the onions into the crust. Pour the egg mixture over the onions.

7. Bake for 50 minutes to 1 hour, until the center of the pie feels firm to the touch. Let sit for 15 minutes before serving. Leftovers are excellent.

Leek and Feta Quiche

This is such an easy dish to make. The only fussy part is making sure to wash the leeks well, as they can be sandy. To clean leeks, cut off the bottom just above the roots, and also cut off the top where the leaves get tough (usually where the color changes to a darker green). Then slice down the length of the leek to the center, but not all the way through. Hold the leek upright under running water, fanning it open, and rinse thoroughly. To dice, slice lengthwise all the way through several times, then turn the leeks and slice horizontally.

Makes 8 servings

1 tablespoon olive oil

½ cup chopped leeks

½ cup diced red bell pepper

5 large eggs

1½ cups milk

¾ cup crumbled feta cheese
   (4 ounces)

½ teaspoon salt

¼ teaspoon freshly ground
   black pepper

1 prebaked 9-inch All-Purpose Pastry
   Crust (page 155)

1. Preheat the oven to 325°F.

2. Heat the olive oil in a medium skillet over medium heat. Sauté the leeks and red bell pepper until softened. Let cool to lukewarm.

3. Whisk together the eggs and milk in a medium bowl. Stir in the cheese and the sautéed vegetables. Season with the salt and pepper.

4. Pour the egg mixture into the crust. Bake for 40 minutes or until set and beginning to brown.

Chard and Feta Strata

Select chard with unblemished dark green leaves. Depending on the variety, the stems and veins in the leaves of the chard will vary in color from white to red to orange. Rainbow-hued chard is beautiful but would color this casserole pink, so buy white chard.

Makes 6 servings

1 cup chopped white chard leaves

1 tablespoon olive oil

2 cloves garlic, minced

½ cup chopped red onion

1 large tomato

Nonstick cooking spray

6 large eggs

¼ cup whole milk

2 slices white sandwich bread

1 teaspoon dried oregano

1 teaspoon dried basil

1 teaspoon kosher salt

¼ teaspoon freshly ground black pepper

½ cup crumbled feta cheese

1 tablespoon grated Parmesan cheese

1. Wash the chard leaves very well. Swirl the leaves in several changes of water, lifting them out so that any grit falls to the bottom of the bowl they are being washed in. Cut off and discard the tough main stems. Coarsely chop the leaves.

2. Heat the olive oil in a large, heavy skillet over low heat. Cook the garlic and onion over low heat for 5 minutes. Add the chard and cook until wilted.

3. Slice the tomato in half and then squeeze out and discard the seeds. Dice the tomato. Use 1 cup for this recipe. Add the tomato to the pan and continue to cook until all the vegetables are softened but not mushy. Put the cooked vegetables in a colander and let drain.

4. Preheat the oven to 350°F. Coat a 9-inch round baking dish with nonstick cooking spray. Since this can be served in its casserole, select an attractive dish.

5. Whisk the eggs and milk in a large bowl until combined. Leaving on the crust, cut the bread into ½-inch cubes. Stir the bread, oregano, basil, salt, and pepper into the eggs. Stir in the vegetables and feta cheese.

6. Spread the mixture into the baking dish. Dust with the Parmesan. Bake for 30 to 40 minutes, until puffed and set in the center.

Basil and Mozzarella Tian

A tian is similar to a quiche, but it doesn't have a crust and is unmolded onto a plate. In this version, the mozzarella balls provide small bursts of flavor. Marinated goat cheese balls would also be very good. This tian is slightly smaller than a standard quiche and so is the perfect size for two when you don't want leftovers.

Makes 2 servings

Nonstick cooking spray

5 large eggs

⅔ cup light cream

½ teaspoon kosher salt

¼ teaspoon freshly ground black pepper

6 fresh basil leaves, sliced

6 oil-packed, herb-marinated mozzarella balls (bocconcini)

¼ red bell pepper (fresh or roasted), sliced

1. Preheat the oven to 325°F. Coat a 1½-quart (about 7 inches round) ceramic baking dish with nonstick cooking spray.

2. Using an electric mixer, beat the eggs and cream for 1 minute. Stir in the salt, pepper, and basil leaves. Pour into the baking dish.

3. Spoon the mozzarella balls out of the oil, drain briefly in a mesh sieve, and then distribute them evenly across the tian.

4. Arrange the red bell pepper over the egg mixture.

5. Bake for 30 to 35 minutes, until the center is set and the edges begin to brown. Use a flexible spatula to loosen the tian from the dish. Invert onto a plate, and then invert once more onto a serving dish.

Savory Spinach Cheesecake

This is party food. It's rich, beautiful, and impressive, but just as important, it's easy on the cook. It can be made ahead of time, served either warm or at room temperature, and can be part of a buffet or the highlight of a luncheon. It's sure to become your go-to recipe for entertaining.

Makes 12 servings

1 tablespoon olive oil

1 medium onion, chopped (1 cup)

1 red bell pepper, diced (1 cup)

1 clove garlic, minced

One 10-ounce package frozen chopped spinach, thawed

Nonstick cooking spray

1 cup grated Parmesan cheese

1 cup ricotta cheese

2 packages cream cheese (1 pound total), at room temperature

6 large eggs

½ cup shredded mozzarella cheese, at room temperature

1 teaspoon kosher salt

¼ teaspoon freshly ground black pepper

1. Heat the olive oil over medium heat in a sauté pan. Sauté the onion, red bell pepper, and garlic until the vegetables soften and begin to turn golden.

2. Squeeze the excess water out of the spinach. Some brands of frozen spinach are coarse and will need chopping; others will come finely minced. Stir the spinach into the vegetables and remove from the heat.

3. Preheat the oven to 325°F. Coat a 9-inch springform pan with nonstick cooking spray. Dust 2 tablespoons of the Parmesan on the bottom of the pan.

4. Combine the ricotta, cream cheese, eggs, mozzarella, remaining Parmesan, salt, and pepper in a large bowl until smooth. This can also be done in a blender.

5. Stir the vegetables into the cheese and egg mixture. Pour into the springform pan.

6. Bake for about 1 hour, until set and the center is firm to the touch. Let cool for 5 minutes before removing from the springform pan. Serve warm or at room temperature.

Savory and Sweet Custards and Puddings

Egg yolks, whose job in nature is to feed the chicks developing within eggs, have an equally essential role in the kitchen. The yolk, a complex mixture of fats, minerals, and proteins, is what makes custards silky, golden rich, thick yet smooth, and comforting yet elegant. Some custards are made with milk and cream, and others with none. Some have whole eggs, some don't. But all must have yolks; custard cannot be made with only the whites. Proportions matter. A delicate custard will have 1 egg per 1 cup of milk, and a denser one will have 3 eggs per cup of milk. Extra yolks make for a thicker pudding.

Custards can be tricky. Heat too high and fast and the eggs will curdle; heat too low and the pudding won't thicken. Sugar slows baking time. Custards made with a bit of starch are easier to get right; ones without starch need careful handling. For example, Crème Anglaise (page 137) can go from liquid to scrambled eggs in the blink of an eye. Some recipes require being heated in a gentle water bath or a double boiler, but others can be made directly in the pot.

All this being said, don't hesitate to try these recipes! Most are truly easy to make, and for the touchier ones, I've built in a margin of error and provided careful directions.

Cheese Custards

Custards aren't just for dessert. Savory custards baked in ramekins can be served chilled with a selection of salads and good bread, or unmolded while still hot and placed onto a pool of tomato sauce. I like to warm up leftovers and spread them on toast for breakfast.

Makes 6 servings

Nonstick cooking spray

4 large eggs

1¾ cups half-and-half

½ teaspoon kosher salt

4 ounces cheese of your choice, grated (1 cup)

2 tablespoons grated Parmesan cheese (optional)

1. Ramekins, which are small ceramic or glass baking dishes, come in various sizes that range from 4 to 8 ounces. Use any size that you have, keeping in mind that an appropriate portion size for this recipe is 6 ounces. You will need 6 to 8 ramekins. Coat them with nonstick spray.

2. Preheat the oven to 350°F.

3. The custards are baked in a water bath, so set the ramekins into a baking dish large enough so that they don't touch. Bring a kettle of water to a boil.

4. Whisk the eggs and half-and-half in a medium bowl. Stir in the salt and the 1 cup grated cheese. Pour this mixture into the ramekins, filling not quite to the rims. If desired, dust with the Parmesan.

5. Put the baking dish into the oven and carefully pour in the hot water until it reaches halfway up the ramekins. Bake for 25 to 30 minutes, until the centers of the custards are firmly set.

Goat Cheese and Asparagus Custards

The basic recipe for Cheese Custards (previous page) can be used as a template for any number of savory combinations. In this version, oozing, tangy goat cheese balances out the rich egg base. Texture is important in custards, so the asparagus is cooked until pliable but not mushy. If the spears are fat, then peel the tough skins from their ends before steaming. If the spears are as thin as pencils, peeling isn't necessary.

Makes 6 servings

Nonstick cooking spray

8 ounces asparagus spears

1 teaspoon butter

¼ cup minced shallot (1 medium)

4 large eggs

1¾ cups half-and-half

½ teaspoon kosher salt

4 ounces soft goat cheese, crumbled (½ cup)

1. Preheat the oven to 350°F.

2. Coat six 6-ounce ramekins with nonstick cooking spray. The custards are baked in a water bath, so set the ramekins into a baking dish large enough so that they don't touch. Bring a kettle of water to a boil.

3. Set up a steamer and steam the asparagus until you can bend it but it is not yet soft. Cut into ½-inch pieces. Measure out 1 cup and reserve any remaining asparagus for another use (it can be tossed into a green salad).

4. Melt the butter in a small sauté pan over low heat and cook the shallots until they begin to brown. Divide the asparagus and shallots equally between the ramekins.

5. Whisk the eggs, half-and-half, and salt in a bowl. Pour into the ramekins, filling not quite to the rims.

6. Put the baking dish into the oven and carefully pour in the hot water until it reaches halfway up the ramekins. Bake for 30 to 35 minutes, until the centers of the custards are firmly set.

Classic Sweet Custard

Classic custard is elegant comfort food, made from the most basic of ingredients: milk, eggs, and sugar. It's also the easiest of the custards to make, as you don't have to watch and stir as it thickens on the stovetop. Instead, it sets in the oven. And you can make this in one dish rather than individual ramekins. It's your choice how rich to make it. A light version can be made with 1 percent milk, and it will still be creamy and won't taste like diet food. If you're feeling indulgent, use half-and-half.

Makes 6 servings

3 cups milk

½ teaspoon vanilla extract

4 egg yolks

2 large eggs

1 cup granulated sugar, plus more
   for topping (optional)

1. Preheat the oven to 300°F. The custard can be baked in one 1½-quart baking dish or in individual 6-ounce ramekins. It is baked in a water bath, so you'll need a pan large enough for the custard dishes to fit into. Bring a kettle of water to a boil.

2. Heat the milk in a small saucepan until just about to boil. Remove from the heat and stir in the vanilla.

3. In a heatproof bowl, whisk the egg yolks, eggs, and sugar. Whisk only enough to dissolve the sugar, not so vigorously that you create air bubbles.

4. Slowly add the hot milk, starting with a small amount so that the eggs don't curdle. Continue to pour in the milk, whisking until smooth.

5. Pour through a fine-mesh sieve into the baking dish. (If making these in individual ramekins, strain into a glass measuring cup and then divide the custard between the dishes.)

6. Put the custard dish into the baking pan and place into the oven. Carefully pour enough of the water from the kettle into the pan to come halfway up the sides of the custard dish. Bake for 45 to 50 minutes, until set. (In the ramekins, it would take about 25 minutes.)

7. Serve as it, or add a sugar topping. To do this, chill the custard in the refrigerator. Right before serving, dust the surface with a fine, even layer of sugar. Using a kitchen torch, sweep the flame over the sugar until it browns, bubbles, and forms a crusty layer of sweetness.

Ginger Pots de Crème

In a first test of this recipe, using standard proportions for this classic French dessert, the farmstead egg yolks masked the delicate flavor of the fresh ginger. I adjusted the recipe, using more fresh ginger and adding crystallized ginger. One other trick is to use salt to enhance the flavor. The end result is a smooth, flavorful custard.

Makes 6 servings

One 2-inch piece fresh ginger

1½ cups whole milk

1 cup heavy cream

1 tablespoon minced crystallized ginger

2 egg yolks

2 large eggs

⅓ cup granulated sugar

¼ teaspoon kosher salt

6 small pieces crystallized ginger

1. Peel the fresh ginger and slice it thinly. Put it in a pot with the milk and cream. Bring to a boil and then immediately turn off the heat. Pour it into a bowl and let it steep for 30 minutes to develop flavor. Let cool to room temperature.

2. Preheat the oven to 300°F. Bring a kettle of water to a boil.

3. Put six 6- to 8-ounce ramekins in a baking dish. (I use a roasting pan because the handles make it safe to move from oven to counter.) Distribute the minced crystallized ginger evenly among the ramekins.

4. In a medium bowl, whisk the yolks, eggs, sugar, and salt. Pour the milk mixture into the eggs. Gently whisk (don't make bubbles) until combined. Strain this mixture through a fine-mesh sieve into a measuring cup or bowl with a lip. Discard the fresh ginger. Pour the mixture into the ramekins.

5. Place the baking dish in the oven. Pour the hot water around the ramekins until it comes halfway up their sides.

6. Bake for 30 to 40 minutes, until the custards are set but slightly wobbly in their centers. Take the baking dish out of the oven and carefully remove the ramekins from the water bath. Place a piece of crystallized ginger on top of each ramekin. Let cool on a wire rack, cover with plastic wrap, and refrigerate. These will keep for 2 days.

Chocolate Bread Pudding

I've made this with several types of bread, from hearty white bread to challah to Portuguese sweet bread. The challah makes a firm pudding. The Portuguese bread is soft and light, so the bread almost disappears into the pudding. As long as a good-quality home-style loaf of bread is used, the pudding will be good. The size and shape of the casserole dish also matters. A deep round casserole will produce a pudding that is soft and gooey in the center. A shallow oblong casserole will produce a pudding that is firmer throughout. This pudding can also be baked in individual portions in 6-ounce ramekins.

Makes 10 servings

Nonstick cooking spray

One 1-pound loaf white bread (unsliced)

3 cups milk (1% or richer)

½ cup granulated sugar

¼ teaspoon kosher salt

8 ounces bittersweet or semisweet chocolate, broken into pieces

1 teaspoon vanilla extract

6 large eggs

½ cup bittersweet chocolate chips

1. Coat a 3-quart baking dish with nonstick cooking spray. Cut the bread into cubes.

2. Combine the milk, sugar, and salt in a medium saucepan. Whisk over medium heat until the sugar dissolves. Increase the heat and bring almost to a simmer. Remove from the heat and stir in the chocolate pieces. Continue to stir gently until the chocolate has melted and the mixture is smooth. Stir in the vanilla.

3. In another bowl, whisk the eggs. When the chocolate mixture has cooled to lukewarm, slowly pour the eggs into the pot, stirring with a whisk until combined.

4. Put the bread cubes in the casserole. Pour the chocolate-egg mixture over the bread and press down on the bread so that it sinks into the batter. Distribute the chocolate chips on top. Cover tightly and refrigerate for a few hours or up to 1 day. This gives the bread time to absorb all of the batter evenly.

5. Pour 1 inch of water into a large pan and set it in the oven. (I like to use a roasting pan because the handles make it easier to take out of the oven later.) Preheat the oven to 350°F. While the oven is preheating, allow the bread pudding to come to room temperature on the counter.

6. Place the casserole in the hot water bath and bake, uncovered, for 50 minutes to 1 hour, until the pudding is set but still soft. (If using ramekins, bake for 30 to 40 minutes.)

Apple Clafoutis

Clafoutis is a dessert that is a bit hard to describe. It's like a sophisticated bread pudding, or a rustic custard. The classic French version is made with cherries. This one has apples sautéed in brandy and then baked into the batter. Top with whipped cream or Crème Anglaise (page 137) and no one will care what you call it, because they'll be too busy savoring every bite!

Makes 6 generous servings

3 large eggs

1¼ cups whole milk

1 teaspoon vanilla extract

⅔ cup all-purpose flour

½ cup plus 1 teaspoon granulated sugar

½ teaspoon kosher salt

2 tablespoons unsalted butter

3 apples, peeled, cored, and sliced

2 tablespoons light brown sugar

2 tablespoons brandy (preferably apple, such as applejack)

¼ teaspoon ground cinnamon

1. Mix the eggs, milk, vanilla, flour, ½ cup of the granulated sugar, and the salt in a blender. Set aside.

2. Preheat the oven to 350°F. Butter a 9-inch deep-dish pie plate or casserole.

3. Heat the butter in a large skillet over medium heat and sauté the apples until they just begin to soften at the edges. Add the brown sugar and cook until the sugar dissolves. Add the brandy. Continue to cook until the apples are softened but the centers remain firm.

4. Arrange the apples evenly on the bottom of the baking dish. Pour the batter over.

5. Combine the cinnamon and the remaining 1 teaspoon granulated sugar. Sprinkle over the batter. Bake for 40 to 45 minutes, until browned and set.

Honey Noodle Kugel

Honey noodle kugel is sweet enough for dessert but is traditionally served at festive holiday meals as an accompaniment to a meat course, such as brisket or roasted chicken. It's ideal on a family reunion buffet table because adults and kids love it equally. It can be served hot, but it can also be offered at room temperature. It cuts into tidy squares that small children like to take right off the serving platter.

Makes 10 servings

8 ounces wide egg noodles

Nonstick cooking spray

8 ounces reduced-fat or regular cream cheese, softened

1 cup reduced-fat or regular sour cream

½ cup clover honey

4 large eggs

½ teaspoon kosher salt

⅛ teaspoon ground cinnamon

1. Bring a large pot of salted water to a boil and cook the noodles until they are pliable but not soft, about 7 minutes. Drain and rinse.

2. Preheat the oven to 350°F. Coat a 9- by 13-inch baking dish with nonstick cooking spray. (Or use a 2½-quart oblong baking casserole and add 10 minutes to the baking time.)

3. Using an electric mixer, beat the cream cheese and sour cream together until smooth. Pour in the honey and beat until combined.

4. Add the eggs, 1 at a time, beating after each addition. Stir in the salt.

5. Stir the noodles gently into the batter so that they are well coated. Break apart any clumps of cooked noodles.

6. Spread the mixture in the baking dish and dust with the cinnamon. Bake for 30 to 35 minutes, until the kugel sets into a soft custard and the top is golden but not browned.

Vanilla Pudding

Is there a dessert more versatile than vanilla pudding? I think not. Its unadorned simplicity is silky, smooth, rich, and comforting. It can be dressed up with berries and freshly whipped cream or dressed down with sliced bananas and animal crackers for a late-night snack.

Makes 6 servings

3 cups milk (your choice from 1% to whole)

⅔ cup granulated sugar

⅛ teaspoon kosher salt

¼ cup cornstarch

4 egg yolks

2 teaspoons vanilla extract

1. Pour 1 cup of the milk into a medium heatproof bowl. Add the sugar, salt, and cornstarch. Stir to dissolve the sugar. Whisk in the egg yolks until smooth.

2. Pour the remaining 2 cups milk into a saucepan. A pot with a rounded bottom edge is best but not necessary. Warm the milk until small bubbles form along the walls of the saucepan.

3. Pour a steady stream of about half of the warm milk into the egg mixture, stirring constantly. (This step prevents the egg from curdling on the stove in the next step.)

4. Pour the egg mixture into the pot. Place on the stove and bring to a simmer. As soon as you see bubbles, set a timer for 2 minutes. Using a heatproof rubber spatula, stir constantly, and scrape along the bottom to prevent sticking. The pudding should bubble but not erupt into splatters. If heated too gently, it won't thicken; if the heat is too high, it will scorch. After 2 minutes it will coalesce into a smooth custard. Stir in the vanilla.

5. Pour the pudding into a fine-mesh sieve set over a bowl. Press with the spatula to push it through the sieve. What remains behind are any little bits of egg white and lumps. Although the pudding will be delicious without this step, straining the pudding is what creates the perfect silky consistency.

6. Chill the pudding in the refrigerator. To prevent a skin from forming, cover with plastic wrap that touches the surface of the pudding.

Lemon Curd

Lemon curd can be eaten as you would jam—spread on toast or dolloped onto a scone. It is also a component of recipes like the Pavlova on page 153, and it can be used as a filling for tartlets—scoop into small prebaked tart shells and top with fresh berries.

Makes 2 cups

3 large eggs

2 egg yolks

¾ cup granulated sugar

⅛ teaspoon kosher salt

½ cup lemon juice, strained (from 3 or 4 lemons)

6 tablespoons unsalted butter

1 teaspoon grated lemon zest

1. Whisk the eggs, egg yolks, sugar, and salt in a heatproof bowl until smooth. Whisk in the lemon juice.

2. Bring a pot of water to a simmer and set the bowl over the simmering water. Using a rubber spatula, stir constantly and heat until the surface roils but doesn't boil. Add the butter, a tablespoon at a time until each is melted. Keep stirring until the mixture thickens and thickly coats the back of a spoon (it will leave a line when you draw your finger through it).

3. Stir in the zest and transfer the curd to a storage container. Refrigerate until ready to use. This keeps for several days.

STRAINING CUSTARDS AND PUDDINGS

Chalazae are opaque white strands that hold the yolk in the center of the egg. A fresh, farmstead egg will have pronounced chalazae. Old eggs and supermarket eggs have faint or nonexistent chalazae. The first time that you crack open an egg from your own hens, you might think that something is wrong! But actually, there is something amiss with the supermarket eggs that don't have chalazae, as these strands are a sign of both freshness and healthy chickens. In years past, French chefs advised leaving eggs out to age before using them for omelets so that the chalazae would fade. I once worked for a chef who insisted that we remove the chalazae by straining the eggs through a sieve before using them for omelets. In my own kitchen, I don't mind the chalazae in omelets or scrambled eggs, but I don't want tough strands in my custards! That is why I've included straining through a fine-mesh sieve in the directions of many of these recipes.

Crème Anglaise

Crème anglaise is a thin, pourable, rich, and decadent custard. A little goes a long way. Although this recipe makes a generous amount, it won't go to waste. Squiggle a line of it on a plate with a slice of chocolate tart. Drizzle it on a clafoutis. Pour it over a bowl of berries. Or, sneak a spoonful straight out of the container. It's that good.

Makes 1½ cups

4 egg yolks

¼ cup granulated sugar

⅛ teaspoon kosher salt

2 teaspoons vanilla extract

1 cup whole milk

¼ cup cream (heavy or light)

1. Whisk the egg yolks, sugar, salt, and vanilla in a bowl until smooth.

2. Warm the milk and cream in a small saucepan. When it is hot but not simmering, stream about ¼ cup into the egg mixture to temper the yolks so that they don't curdle.

3. Add the cream-yolk mixture to the saucepan and cook over low heat. Stir with a wooden spoon (not a whisk, as you don't want air bubbles) until thick enough to coat the back of the spoon but not as thick as a pudding. If in doubt, use an instant-read thermometer and bring the crème anglaise to 160°F. Do not rush this step, or you'll have scrambled eggs and not a pourable custard!

4. Strain the sauce through a fine-mesh sieve and transfer to a storage container. Refrigerate until ready to use. This keeps for several days.

Eggnog

When you buy eggnog in a carton at the supermarket, it doesn't much remind you of eggs. Rather it's like drinking spiced, sweetened cream. I much prefer this homemade version that showcases the good flavor and yellow yolks of the eggs from my hens. I even make this drink with all whole milk and no cream because I like the thinner consistency, but for classic nog, use light cream and serve in small punch glasses.

Makes 7 cups (about 14 servings)

4 cups whole milk

6 large eggs

⅓ cup granulated sugar

1 teaspoon vanilla extract

1 cup light cream

½ cup brandy or rum

1 teaspoon ground cinnamon

¼ teaspoon ground nutmeg

¼ teaspoon ground cloves

1. Warm the milk in a saucepan until hot but not simmering. Meanwhile, whisk the eggs and sugar in a heatproof bowl until well mixed and a warm yellow color.

2. Pour about ½ cup of the hot milk into the eggs and whisk. Then slowly add the milk-egg mixture to the pot and return to the stovetop.

3. Bring the mixture to a gentle simmer. If you rush this step and use high heat, the eggs will curdle, so take your time. Stir constantly until the mixture coats the back of the spoon and a finger run along the spoon leaves a clear trail. If you have one, use an instant-read thermometer and cook until it reaches 160°F.

4. Strain through a fine-mesh sieve. Straining is essential to make this the perfect smooth consistency for drinking, as this step will remove the chalazae and any small lumps. Refrigerate the eggnog until thoroughly chilled. This can be made at least a day ahead of time.

5. When ready to serve, stir in the vanilla, cream, and brandy. Mix the cinnamon, nutmeg, and cloves and put in a small shaker or a bowl with a spoon. To serve, pour the eggnog into a glass and dust with the spices.

Mayonnaise and Sauces

A miraculous alchemy happens when egg yolks are whipped with oil and lemon juice: They transform into a silken, billowy, rich, and savory spread. There's science behind why this happens, but each time I whip up mayonnaise, it seems like magic.

Mayonnaise is a sauce that is created by holding together two very different liquids (in this case lemon juice and oil) by beating them into droplets, and then keeping them from separating with the help of an emulsifier. Egg yolks happen to be superb at this task. Bottled commercial sauces use a myriad of chemical emulsifiers to keep ingredients in suspension, but at home, wholesome, flavorful yolks are all that is needed to make perfect and luscious mayonnaise.

Real mayonnaise, because it is made with raw egg yolks, needs to be kept refrigerated until use. When brought to the table, it's best to set the serving bowl on another bowl filled with ice. At picnics, keep mayonnaise-dressed salads chilled in a cooler. But don't hesitate to make and use it! Real, homemade mayonnaise is one of the nicest indulgences to have, especially when you have good farmstead eggs. Mayonnaise is the most basic version of this emulsification. Add garlic and you have aioli.

Mayonnaise

If you've never had homemade mayonnaise, how good it is will surprise you. The color will, too: It's yellow, not white like the jarred version. There are few lunches better than a homegrown-tomato and bacon sandwich made with fresh mayonnaise.

Makes 1 cup

1 large egg

2 egg yolks

1 teaspoon Dijon mustard

1 tablespoon lemon juice

½ teaspoon kosher salt

⅛ teaspoon freshly ground black pepper

¾ cup vegetable oil

1. Put the egg, egg yolks, mustard, lemon juice, salt, and pepper in a medium bowl and whisk until thick.

2. While whisking constantly, add the oil in a slow, steady stream and continue to whisk until thick. (The mayonnaise will begin to separate after about a day. A brisk whisking will thicken it up again.) Use within 3 days.

Aioli

Aioli is garlicky, lemony homemade mayonnaise. It is rich, smooth, and pungent. It is great as a dip for crudités, a sauce for steamed vegetables, a spread for sandwiches (try it on fried egg and tomato), or a dipping sauce for grilled fish skewers (page 142). Because aioli is made with raw egg yolks, it is important to keep it refrigerated and serve it chilled. When it is to be served at a buffet where it would be left out long enough to reach room temperature, eliminate worries by setting the bowl of aioli in a bowl filled with ice.

Makes 1 cup

4 cloves garlic, peeled

½ teaspoon kosher salt

2 egg yolks

1 teaspoon Dijon mustard

¼ teaspoon freshly ground white or black pepper

3 teaspoons lemon juice

1 cup extra-virgin olive oil

1. Using a chef's knife, mash and mince the garlic with the salt until you get a smooth paste.

2. In a small bowl, whisk the garlic paste and egg yolks. Add the mustard and pepper, and whisk until smooth. Whisk in 1 teaspoon of the lemon juice.

3. Add half of the oil in a slow, steady stream, whisking vigorously until thick. Stir in the remaining 2 teaspoons lemon juice, and then finish whisking in the oil.

Swordfish Kabobs with Aioli

Use this recipe as a jumping-off point for other kabobs. Aioli is good on grilled chicken and beef, too. Not only can you vary the meats, but you can, of course, get creative with the vegetables. During corn season, skewer pieces of corn on the cob. Kabobs are charming made with pattypan squash. In fact, make a few kabobs with just fresh produce from the garden or farmer's market. Dipped in aioli, even confirmed meat-eaters will enjoy their vegetables.

Makes 4 servings

FOR THE KABOBS:

2 small summer squash, sliced into
   1-inch pieces

1 pint cherry tomatoes

2 green bell peppers, cut into
   large pieces

1 red onion, cut into large pieces

1 pound swordfish, cut into
   large cubes

FOR THE DRESSING:

¼ cup olive oil

2 tablespoons lemon juice

½ teaspoon kosher salt

½ teaspoon freshly ground
   black pepper

FOR SERVING:

1 recipe aioli (page 141)

1.   To make the kabobs: Assemble the skewers by adding the items in this order until all have been used: squash, tomato, pepper, onion, swordfish, onion, squash, tomato, and so forth.

2.   To make the dressing: Whisk all of the ingredients together. Pour over the skewers to coat. These can be refrigerated for up to a day before grilling.

3.   Preheat a grill to medium heat. Grill the kabobs for about 8 minutes, until the swordfish is just cooked through. Turn the kabobs once or twice during grilling. Serve the aioli on the side.

Mayonnaise-Slathered Baked Catfish

This recipe produces very moist baked fish with a crispy exterior. I specified catfish here because it is a firm-fleshed white fish that holds together well when cooked. Another option would be tilapia. Don't use a thick fish like cod, as the outer edges will overcook before the center is done. Do use a mild-flavored fish, as you want to be able to taste the subtle flavor of the homemade mayonnaise.

Makes 3 or 4 servings

Nonstick olive oil cooking spray

⅓ to ½ cup homemade mayonnaise (page 140)

½ cup dry bread crumbs

1 pound skinless catfish fillets

1. Preheat the oven to 375°F. Coat a baking sheet with cooking spray.

2. Put the mayonnaise on a dinner plate and the bread crumbs on another plate.

3. Wash and dry the fillets. Dip a fillet into the mayonnaise and generously coat both sides. Transfer the fish to the plate with the bread crumbs. Dredge the fish in the bread crumbs and then gently shake off any excess. Put the fillet on the baking sheet. Repeat with the remaining fillets.

4. Lightly coat the fish with cooking spray. Bake for 12 to 15 minutes, or until done. You can usually tell when a fish fillet is cooked by the color of the flesh and how it flakes apart. Since you don't want to pry apart a breaded fillet, however, to test for doneness touch the center of the fillet with your finger. If it feels as firm as the bottom of the palm of your hand, it is done.

Meringues and Soufflés

Egg whites are almost pure protein, and yet they whip up into magic. Whites from fresh eggs are stronger and hold their shape better than the thin and watery whites often found in supermarket eggs. I know that

room temperature whites are supposed to beat into higher peaks, but with my fresh eggs I can't say that I can tell the difference! If you're not experienced with egg whites, I suggest that you sacrifice a couple to an experiment. Put them in a bowl and, using an electric mixer (best is a stand mixer with a balloon whisk), start beating. Notice when they froth. Pay attention to when they start to take shape. Start and stop the beaters and see when the peaks fold over, and then what it looks like when they stay stiffly upright. Then, keep beating until

they go dry and break. Once you've seen all of the stages of whipped egg whites, you'll be better able (and braver) about beating them until the moment they are at their best.

Whipped egg whites—glossy, white, and firm but not brittle—are the secret to so many good foods. They give soufflés that ethereal quality, they make angel food cake light, they form billowy toppings to pies, and with a hint of flavoring they make meringues melt-in-your-mouth delicious.

Cheese Soufflé

Use this recipe as a fail-safe guide to making savory soufflés. You can add in things like minced ham, grated carrots, goat cheese, sun-dried tomatoes, chopped walnuts, spinach, or feta. Don't let the word "soufflé" scare you. The secret about soufflés is that even if they fall, they still taste good! However, it's important to handle the batter gently. One folds the egg whites into the base, one never stirs! This careful technique insures that the whites hold the air beaten into them, and that the soufflé emerges from the oven light and ethereal.

Makes 4 servings

1 cup whole milk

3 tablespoons unsalted butter

3 tablespoons all-purpose flour

½ teaspoon paprika

½ teaspoon kosher salt

⅛ teaspoon freshly ground black pepper

⅛ teaspoon ground nutmeg

6 large eggs, separated, at room temperature

1 cup shredded Swiss cheese

1. Preheat the oven to 375°F. Put the rack in the lower third of the oven. Butter a 1½-quart soufflé dish. In the microwave or in a small saucepan, warm the milk until hot but not simmering.

2. In a medium saucepan, melt the butter. Stir in the flour and cook for 2 minutes, until bubbly but not brown. Slowly pour in the hot milk while whisking vigorously. Increase the heat and boil for about 3 minutes, until the mixture thickens. Remove from the heat and scrape into a large bowl. Stir in the paprika, salt, pepper, and nutmeg and let cool slightly.

3. When the flour mixture is slightly warmer than room temperature, stir in the egg yolks, one at a time. (This base can be made up to a day ahead of time and stored in the refrigerator.)

4. In a clean bowl, using an electric mixer, beat the egg whites and a pinch of salt on high speed until stiff peaks form.

5. Scoop out ¼ cup of the egg whites and stir it into the base. Then add the rest of the whites to the base. Gently fold these two mixtures together, adding ¼ cup of the cheese at a time until fully combined.

6. Spoon the filling into the soufflé dish. Bake for 35 minutes, or until the soufflé rises and forms a sloping, crusty cap and wobbles a bit when pushed. The soufflé will begin to deflate within 3 minutes of being removed from the oven, so bring it right to the table and serve immediately.

Chocolate Soufflé

Two of my favorite ingredients—eggs and chocolate—combine in this recipe to create a perfect dessert. Made with unsweetened chocolate, this soufflé is an intense chocolate experience. But you can use semisweet chocolate if preferred.

Makes 4 servings

6 tablespoons plus 1 teaspoon granulated sugar

2 ounces unsweetened chocolate, broken into pieces

1 tablespoon water

2 tablespoons unsalted butter

⅛ teaspoon kosher salt

2 tablespoons all-purpose flour

¾ cup whole milk

3 large eggs, separated

1 teaspoon vanilla extract

1. Preheat the oven to 325°F. Butter a 1½-quart soufflé dish and dust with 1 teaspoon of the sugar.

2. Combine the chocolate, 3 tablespoons of the sugar, and the water in a small saucepan. Melt the chocolate over very low heat, stirring frequently until smooth. Set aside.

3. Melt the butter in a small pot. Stir in the salt and flour, and whisk constantly for 1 minute. Slowly pour in the milk and continue to whisk. Bring to a boil, then immediately lower the heat to a gentle simmer and whisk for 2 minutes, until thickened. Remove the pot from the heat and scrape the contents into a bowl.

4. Add the chocolate mixture to the bowl with the milk. Stir until well blended.

5. In a separate bowl, whisk the egg yolks until smooth. Scoop a little of the hot chocolate mixture into the bowl with the yolks and blend. Then stir all the yolks into the chocolate mixture. Stir in the vanilla.

6. Using an electric mixer, beat the egg whites on high speed until foamy. Add the remaining 3 tablespoons sugar and beat until stiff.

7. Put one-third of the whites into the bowl with the chocolate and stir until combined. Then take one-quarter of the chocolate mixture and, using a sweeping, folding motion, blend the whites with the chocolate. Continue to add large dollops of egg whites until they are all folded into the chocolate. Done in these increments, the soufflé's airy texture is preserved.

8. Spoon the batter into the soufflé dish. Bake in the center of the oven for 30 to 35 minutes, until the soufflé has risen and is only a bit wobbly in the center when the dish is jiggled.

Chocolate-Kahlúa Volcanoes

These "volcanoes" are the sort of impressive, absolutely delicious dessert that causes conversation to stop as guests taste their first spoonful. Like soufflés, they rise and fall, but unlike soufflés, only egg whites are used.

Makes 4 servings

2 tablespoons plus 2 teaspoons granulated sugar

4 ounces bittersweet or semisweet chocolate, broken into 1-ounce or smaller pieces

½ cup whipping cream

1 tablespoon Kahlúa

4 egg whites

1. Preheat the oven to 400°F. Butter four 6- or 8-ounce ramekins. Dust them with 2 teaspoons of the sugar. Set on a baking sheet.

2. Warm (do not boil) the chocolate and cream in the microwave or in a small saucepan. Heat until the chocolate melts and the mixture begins to thicken. Stir in the Kahlúa, then let cool. Set aside ⅓ cup of this mixture.

3. With an electric mixer, whip the egg whites on high speed until foamy. Keep beating while you gradually add the remaining 2 tablespoons sugar. Continue to whip on high speed until the egg whites become stiff.

4. Take a big dollop from the main bowl of the chocolate mixture and fold it into the egg whites. Continue to add the chocolate, folding it gently into the egg whites until all but the reserved ⅓ cup has been combined with the egg whites. Spoon this egg white mixture into the ramekins.

5. Divide the reserved ⅓ cup of chocolate evenly among the ramekins, putting a large spoonful on top in the center of each one.

6. Bake for about 12 minutes, until puffed and set.

ABOUT MERINGUES

There are three types of meringues. Of them, the Italian meringue is more for the professional baker and used for shelf-stable pie toppings and frostings. It requires cooking sugar to the soft-ball stage, and I don't use it here. However, the other two meringues, called French and Swiss, have a multitude of uses and, once you are comfortable with the technique, are quite useful.

The French meringue is the most basic. It is simply egg whites beaten with a little acid (cream of tartar usually serves that purpose, although some cooks use vinegar). The acid helps to stabilize the egg foam. For sweet meringues, sugar is slowly poured into the bowl as the eggs are being whipped. Soon they are white, shiny, and voluminous. An angel food cake is simply a French meringue combined with flour.

The Swiss meringue is similar to the French, except that the egg whites are first heated over boiling water. Those worried about the dangers of eating uncooked eggs might want to use Swiss meringues. They also whip up stiffer than the French and so are better for frostings. When stability is important, more sugar is added, as that improves the structure by pulling water out of the egg white foam.

Chocolate-Walnut Meringue Cookies

This is my favorite way to use up extra egg whites. In fact, these work equally well when made with frozen egg whites. Simply defrost the whites in the refrigerator and then follow the recipe.

Makes 18 to 20 cookies

4 ounces bittersweet or semisweet chocolate

3 egg whites

⅛ teaspoon cream of tartar

¾ cup granulated sugar

1 cup finely chopped walnuts (4 ounces)

1. Preheat the oven to 300°F. Line two baking sheets with parchment paper.

2. Break the chocolate into small pieces and melt it in the microwave, using low power. Stir until smooth, and let cool.

3. With an electric mixer, beat the egg whites and cream of tartar on high speed until soft peaks form. With the machine running, add ½ cup of the sugar, 1 tablespoon at a time. Beat until shiny and very stiff peaks form.

4. Using a spatula, fold in the remaining ¼ cup sugar and then the chocolate. Stir gently. You don't have to mix it perfectly; thin streaks of egg whites and chocolate can remain. Stir in the walnuts until distributed throughout.

5. Using two teaspoons, drop large dollops of meringue onto the baking sheets, spacing them about 3 inches apart.

6. Bake for 20 to 25 minutes, rotating the baking sheets halfway through, until the cookies form a light, dry exterior but have a slightly soft (chewy) center.

Lemon Kisses

These are the same size and shape as chocolate kisses but are melt-in-your-mouth pillows of lemony sweetness.

Lemon zest—the yellow peel without the bitter white pith—is a key component of this recipe. The easiest way to get finely shredded zest is to run a Microplane grater over the surface of the lemon. The Microplane is one of those tools that, once you have it, will make you wonder how you ever worked without it. If you don't have a Microplane, then use a vegetable peeler (a sharp peeler will remove the zest without the pith) and very finely mince.

Makes 100 kisses

½ cup egg whites (about 6 whites)

½ teaspoon cream of tartar

⅔ cup granulated sugar

1 teaspoon lemon juice

1 teaspoon vanilla extract

2 teaspoons finely grated lemon zest

1. Preheat the oven to 200°F. Line baking sheets with parchment paper.

2. Using an electric mixer, beat the egg whites and cream of tartar on high speed until foamy.

3. With the mixer running, slowly stream in half of the sugar. Pour in the lemon juice and vanilla. Gradually add the rest of the sugar, beating until stiff and glossy peaks form.

4. Quickly whisk in the lemon zest.

5. Using a pastry bag with a star tip, pipe kisses (the size of the chocolate candy of the same name) onto the baking sheets. These will not spread, so you can put them close together. If you don't want to fuss with a pastry bag, use a teaspoon to scoop out the meringue and another to scrape it onto the parchment. These will have irregular and charming surfaces.

6. Bake for 2½ hours, until dry. If they are still chewy, keep baking until crisp; depending on the weather, this can possibly take another hour. Turn off the oven, leave the door ajar, and let sit for an hour. Do not attempt this recipe on a humid day, as these have to be so dry that they shatter in the mouth when eaten. Store in an airtight container for up to 2 days.

Pavlova with Lemon Curd Whipped Cream

I have a friend who grew up in Australia, and this is the one food from her childhood that she reminisces about. It's the sort of recipe that a child could be entranced by and yet an adult would feel sophisticated eating. It is sweet, billowy, dramatic, and ethereal. It's also surprisingly easy to whip up. The base is a basic meringue, and the lemon curd can be made up to a week in advance— just don't eat it all before making the Pavlova!

Makes 8 servings

½ cup egg whites (about 6 whites)

½ teaspoon cream of tartar

⅔ cup granulated sugar

1 cup heavy cream

1 cup Lemon Curd (page 136)

1 cup fresh berries of your choice

1. Preheat the oven to 250°F. Trace a 12-inch circle onto a sheet of parchment paper (I use a large dinner plate). Turn the paper ink side down onto a baking sheet.

2. With an electric mixer, beat the egg whites on high speed until foamy. Add the cream of tartar and mix until the eggs start to hold their shape.

3. With the mixer running, add the sugar in a slow, steady stream. Continue to whip at high speed until the egg whites are stiff and glossy and when you stop the beaters, an egg white peak holds its shape without falling over.

4. Using a rubber spatula, spread the meringue into the parchment circle, building up the outside edge a tad higher. If you are comfortable working with a pastry bag, this can be piped in.

5. Bake the meringue for 1 to 1½ hours, until dry. Turn off the oven, crack the door open, and let the meringue continue to dry for an hour. When done, the meringue will sound hollow when tapped and it will peel easily off the parchment. If the weather is humid, extend the baking time until the meringue is dry.

6. Peel off the parchment and place the cooked meringue on a serving dish. Unless the weather is damp, the meringue can be made a day in advance and kept at room temperature.

7. Using an electric mixer, beat the cream until full and stiff. Using a rubber spatula, gently stir in the lemon curd until no yellow streaks remain visible. Spread this mixture into the meringue shell, leaving the higher edges bare.

8. Arrange the fruit on top. Serve immediately.

Sweet Pies and Tarts

If I were limited to only one food that I could cook, it would be pies, and eggs would be in all of them. In some pies, eggs are the main event. Oh, how I love custard pies! Top off a custard pie with frothy, sweet meringue, and you have layers of eggy goodness (the epitome of this is the Lemon Meringue Pie on page 158). Eggs also form the base and add silken texture to such luscious delights as Chocolate Tart (page 162). Sometimes, eggs can be the unnoticed binder in a recipe like the Cranberry-Nut Tart (page 166). However the eggs are used, it's always a good time for pie.

All-Purpose Pastry Crusts

All-butter pastry crusts taste wonderful, but they are softer and not as flaky as those made with solid shortening. I used to shy away from shortening because of the off flavor and the trans fats. Now, however, you can buy solid shortening without hydrogenated fats. You can even find an organic version. If you want, you can also make this with all butter. Use 1½ sticks of butter and no shortening. The rest of the recipe remains the same.

Makes 2 single crusts for 9- to 10-inch pie plates

½ cup (1 stick) unsalted butter, frozen (not just chilled)

5 to 6 tablespoons ice water

2 cups all-purpose flour

½ teaspoon kosher salt

⅓ cup solid shortening, chilled

1. This crust is made in a food processor fitted with the steel blade. The trick to a perfect crust is to use the pulse button. Never let the machine run for more than about 3 seconds at a time. Also, start with frozen butter. If you plan ahead, measure out and freeze the shortening as well. Using a chef's knife, cut the frozen butter in half lengthwise, then slice it into ½ inch pieces. Have a measuring cup with the ice water ready.

2. Put the flour, salt, and butter in the processor bowl. Pulse until all is crumbly. Add the solid shortening. Pulse in brief spurts until the fats are in small pieces and evenly distributed throughout the flour.

3. Add the water, 1 tablespoon at a time, pulsing the machine in 3-second bursts after each addition. The dough should start to ball up. At this point, remove it from the machine.

4. Pat the dough into a solid ball. Divide it in half and shape each half into a flattened round. If the dough is still very cold, then it can be rolled out immediately. But on a warm day, wrap tightly with plastic wrap and refrigerate for at least 30 minutes before rolling it out. The dough can be frozen, wrapped in plastic and then in aluminum foil, for up to 2 months. If frozen, thaw overnight in the refrigerator before using.

5. To roll out the dough, dust your countertop with flour. Using a rolling pin, push down on the dough, starting at the center and

Continued on next page

Continued from previous page

using outward strokes, lifting and turning the dough after every few pushes to make sure it doesn't stick and to keep it even all around.

6. When the dough is about 11 inches in diameter, fold it in half and then in half again so that it looks like a quarter of a pie. Place this in the pie plate and unfold. Trim off the ragged excess so that about 1 inch overhangs the edge of the pie plate. Tuck the over-hanging dough under itself all the way around the edge so it just extends past the edge. Next, flute or press with a fork to decorate the edges.

7. If partial prebaking is called for, preheat the oven to 375°F. Place a piece of nonstick aluminum foil on the crust, loosely covering the edges of the pie. Weight down with pie weights or dry uncooked beans. Bake until golden and the edges begin to brown, 12 to 15 minutes.

8. For recipes that call for putting a precooked custard or other chilled filling into a fully baked crust, after prebaking with the weights, remove the foil and weights and continue to bake until the crust is lightly golden in the center.

Graham Cracker Crust

Those store-bought graham cracker crusts are convenient, but not only are they in small, shallow pie tins, they also don't taste half as good as this homemade version. This crust takes only a couple of minutes to make and is well worth the effort. A good crust elevates any pie to the next level of deliciousness. For example, the Lime Tart (page 159) is a very simple recipe, but combine that sweet-tart filling with this crumbly graham goodness, and you have a dessert greater than the sum of its parts. Graham crackers vary in texture and flavor. Most of the store brands are too sweet, and some (not all) of the natural-food brands taste too much of whole wheat. I stick with the red box that I remember from childhood.

Makes one 9- or 10-inch crust

10 large (4½ by 2¼ inches) graham crackers

2 tablespoons light brown sugar

6 tablespoons unsalted butter, melted

1. Use a food processor to turn the crackers into crumbs. You will get about 1¼ cups of finely ground crumbs.

2. Add the brown sugar and pulse. Add the butter and pulse until the mixture looks like wet sand. Do not let the machine run.

3. Turn out the crumb mixture into a 9- or 10-inch pie plate. Press the mixture along the bottom and up the sides to make a firm and even crust.

4. If prebaking is called for, preheat the oven to 350°F. Bake for 10 minutes. The crust can be made a day ahead of time.

Lemon Meringue Pie

Really good eggs do more than just thicken the filling; they provide a flavor base that mellows and blends the intense tartness of the lemons with the pure sweetness of the sugar. Unlike a custard pie, which requires a watchful eye and careful timing, all these ingredients need is a quick whisk in a bowl. This pie can be prepared in a 9-inch pie plate or a 10-inch tart pan (shallow, with a removable bottom). Note: Prebaking the pie crust is essential! I once tried to skip this step and the crust floated up to the surface and set there as the pie baked. Top with a meringue or nothing at all.

Makes 8 servings

1 All-Purpose Pastry Crust (page 155)
   or Graham Cracker Crust
   (page 157)

3 large eggs

3 egg yolks

½ cup lemon juice

1 cup granulated sugar

½ cup heavy whipping cream

1 teaspoon grated lemon zest

FOR THE MERINGUE TOPPING:

⅔ cup egg whites (4 to 6 whites)

½ cup granulated sugar

½ teaspoon cream of tartar

½ teaspoon vanilla extract

1. Partially prebake the crust of your choice according to the individual recipe directions. Bake until it is only lightly golden, because the crust will brown while the lemon filling bakes and then will bake further if a meringue is used.

2. Preheat the oven to 375°F.

3. Whisk the ingredients together in the order listed: eggs, egg yolks, lemon juice, sugar, whipping cream, and zest. Whisk after each addition so that the batter is thoroughly blended though not bubbly.

4. Pour the filling into the crust and bake for 25 to 30 minutes, until set and slightly golden on the surface. Let the pie cool.

5. Meanwhile, make the meringue. Place the whites and sugar in a heatproof bowl and set over a pot of hot (not boiling) water. Stir gently until the sugar dissolves. Remove the bowl from the pot and stir in the cream of tartar.

6. Using an electric mixer, beat the egg white mixture on high speed until stiff and shiny. Stir in the vanilla.

7. Once the pie is at room temperature, bring the oven back to 375°F. Spread the meringue over the pie filling, making sure it touches the crust (to prevent shrinkage). Place the pie in the oven so that it is about 4 inches from the top heating element. Bake for 8 to 12 minutes until the peaks of the meringue brown lightly.

Lime Tart

This pie is dairy-free, and the filling is gluten-free as well. The simplicity of the ingredients and unfussy preparation belie its bright, complex flavors. It's probably the easiest pie in my repertoire, and in a pinch is very good in a store-bought graham cracker crust.

Makes 8 servings

4 large eggs

3 egg yolks

½ cup lime juice (from about 4 limes)

1¼ cups granulated sugar

1 prebaked 9-inch All-Purpose Pastry Crust (page 155) or Graham Cracker Crust (page 157)

1. Preheat the oven to 350°F.

2. Using a blender, combine the eggs, egg yolks, lime juice, and sugar until smooth.

3. Pour the mixture through a fine-mesh sieve into the crust. (This fussy step of straining is essential for a smooth custard.)

4. Pop the air bubbles on the surface with a toothpick.

5. Bake for 25 to 30 minutes, until the filling is set and the top is a uniform dark golden color. Chill before serving.

Chocolate Cream Pie with Meringue Topping

This pie should be made with the best dark chocolate you can find. Basic chocolate from the baking aisle at the supermarket won't do. It's worth making a special trip to get high-quality chocolate. Use a chocolate between 68 and 78 percent cacao for this.

For a cloud of sweetness on top of your pie, make a meringue topping. Not only will it put the perfect finish on the pie, but it will also use up those extra egg whites. A true meringue topping for pie is delicate and ethereal. The whites whip up to glossy peaks but within a few hours will weep out liquid and begin to collapse. Sure, this doesn't happen to nondairy whipped topping, and those pretty mile-high pies at chain restaurants have stabilizers and other chemicals to keep them aloft, but trust me—you want the real thing. If you like, you may instead top the pie with homemade whipped cream.

Makes 8 servings

8 ounces bittersweet or semisweet chocolate, broken into small pieces

1 tablespoon unsalted butter, melted

1 teaspoon vanilla extract

⅔ cup granulated sugar

¼ cup cornstarch

¼ teaspoon kosher salt

6 egg yolks

3 cups whole milk

1 prebaked 9-inch Graham Cracker Crust (page 157)

FOR THE MERINGUE TOPPING:

⅔ cup egg whites (4 to 6 whites)

½ cup granulated sugar

½ teaspoon cream of tartar

½ teaspoon vanilla extract

1. Melt the chocolate and butter in a heatproof bowl set over simmering water. Stir in the vanilla and set aside.

2. In a medium heavy saucepan, whisk together the sugar, cornstarch, salt, and egg yolks. In a slow, steady stream, add the milk and whisk until well combined.

3. Over medium-high heat, bring the contents to a boil, whisking constantly. Once boiling, time for exactly 1 minute, whisking continually as it thickens. Remove from the heat.

4. Pour this sugar mixture into a fine-mesh sieve and push it through into the bowl with the chocolate. Stir to combine with the chocolate. Cover the surface with plastic wrap, place in the refrigerator, and let cool completely, about 2 hours.

5. Scrape the filling into the crust, cover loosely, and chill for at least 6 hours before serving.

6. To prepare the meringue, preheat the oven to 375°F.

7. Place the egg whites and sugar in a heatproof bowl and set over a pot of hot (not boiling) water. Stir gently until the sugar dissolves. Remove the bowl from the pot and stir in the cream of tartar.

8. Using an electric mixer, beat the egg white mixture on high speed until stiff and shiny. Stir in the vanilla.

9. Spread the meringue over the pie filling, making sure it touches the crust (to prevent shrinkage). Place in the oven about 4 inches from the top heating element. Bake for 8 to 12 minutes, until the peaks of the meringue brown lightly.

Chocolate Tart

This recipe is easy to make and yet impressive. It's perfect as is, but serve it with a squiggle of Crème Anglaise (page 137) and a few fresh raspberries, and it will remind you of the best chocolate dessert you've ever had at a restaurant. The quality and flavor of the chocolate will determine the success of this recipe, so it's worth it to splurge on good chocolate.

Makes 8 servings

6 ounces bittersweet or semisweet chocolate, coarsely chopped

2 tablespoons unsweetened cocoa powder

2 large eggs

3 egg yolks

1 cup heavy cream

½ cup granulated sugar

½ teaspoon vanilla extract

1 prebaked Graham Cracker Crust (page 157) or All-Purpose Pastry Crust (page 155)

1. Melt the chocolate in a double boiler or in the microwave. Let cool to lukewarm. Stir in the cocoa powder.

2. Preheat the oven to 350°F.

3. Whisk the eggs and egg yolks until smooth. Stir in the cream and sugar until well combined. Do not do this so vigorously that you create air bubbles.

4. Using a rubber spatula, stir in the melted chocolate and the vanilla. Stir gently until all is one color and no streaks remain.

5. Spread the chocolate batter into the crust.

6. Bake for 30 to 35 minutes, until firmly set. (I bake this pie set on a baking sheet to ease moving it into and out of the oven.) Let come to room temperature or chill before serving.

Pumpkin Cheesecake

There are many styles of cheesecake. This one is a classic American cream cheese–based version. It's creamy and, of course, rich. You'll need a 10-inch springform pan for the graham cracker crust.

Makes 10 servings

Nonstick cooking spray

1 Graham Cracker Crust (page 157)

Four 8-ounce packages cream
   cheese, at room temperature

1 cup granulated sugar

½ cup light brown sugar

½ cup sour cream

1 teaspoon vanilla extract

6 large eggs

¼ cup pumpkin puree

½ teaspoon ground ginger

1. Preheat the oven to 325°F. Coat a 10-inch springform pan with nonstick cooking spray. Line the bottom with a circle of parchment paper.

2. Press the graham cracker crust into the bottom of the spring-form pan. Bake for 12 minutes. Remove from the oven and let cool.

3. Using an electric mixer, beat the cream cheese and sugars. Add the sour cream and beat until well mixed. Beat in the vanilla and eggs until smooth.

4. Scoop out 1¼ cups of the cheesecake filling and stir it into a bowl along with the pumpkin puree and ginger.

5. Pour the plain cheesecake batter into the springform pan. Pour the pumpkin mixture into the center.

6. Pull a knife through the cheesecake batter, as if slicing the batter into wedges, to marble it. Then pull the knife through the batter in concentric circles.

7. Bake the cake in the center of the oven for 1 hour and 20 minutes, or until the center sets. Let cool slowly on the counter, and then put in the refrigerator and chill before serving.

Peach-Lemon Chiffon Pie

During peach season, it's worth going to the messy trouble of peeling and slicing fresh, juicy peaches for this pie. Out-of-season peaches have no flavor and a mealy texture; I never use them. Instead, I turn to the frozen peach slices available in the supermarket. This is a tall pie; use a deep-dish pie plate if you have one.

Makes 8 servings

2 cups peeled and sliced peaches
(thawed if frozen)

1 envelope (1 tablespoon) unflavored
powdered gelatin

¼ cup water

4 large eggs, separated

1 cup granulated sugar

¼ cup lemon juice

1 teaspoon grated lemon zest

¼ teaspoon kosher salt

1 prebaked 9- or 10-inch Graham
Cracker Crust (page 157)

1. Puree the peach slices. Measure out 1 cup of puree for this recipe.

2. Sprinkle the gelatin over the water and let soften for a few minutes.

3. In a small heavy saucepan, whisk the egg yolks and ¾ cup of the sugar. Place over medium heat and whisk constantly until foamy and hot but not boiling. Stir in the gelatin mixture. Whisk for 30 seconds and then remove from the heat. Scrape into a bowl.

4. Stir the peach puree, lemon juice, and zest into the egg yolk mixture. Refrigerate for about 1½ hours, stirring occasionally, until it becomes the consistency of thick applesauce.

5. With an electric mixer, beat the egg whites and salt until soft peaks form. With the mixer running, slowly add the remaining ¼ cup sugar. Beat until stiff.

6. Gently stir ½ cup of the peach mixture into the egg whites. Then fold the whites into the bowl with the peach mixture until combined.

7. Mound the filling into the crust. Chill for several hours before serving.

Cranberry-Nut Tart

You usually don't think about eggs when you think about pecan pie, but without eggs the corn syrup and brown sugar would harden into an inedible mass. I'm not a big fan of pecan pie; to my taste it is usually cloyingly sugary. This dessert solves the problem by including fresh cranberries. Each mouthful is both tart and sweet. I've also used three types of nuts, which gives this tart a complexity of flavor and texture.

Makes 10 servings

1 All-Purpose Pastry Crust
   (page 155)

3 large eggs

1 cup light brown sugar

½ cup light corn syrup

2 tablespoons unsalted butter,
   melted and cooled to
   room temperature

½ teaspoon kosher salt

1 tablespoon orange liqueur,
   such as Grand Marnier

1 cup fresh or frozen
   whole cranberries

½ cup walnuts (whole or halves)

½ cup pecans (whole or halves)

¼ cup cashews (whole or halves)

1. Pat the crust dough into a 10-inch tart pan (with a removable bottom) or a regular (not deep-dish) 10-inch pie plate. Prebake according to the directions, until lightly golden brown.

2. Meanwhile, using a whisk, combine the eggs, brown sugar, corn syrup, butter, and salt. When smoothly blended, whisk in the orange liqueur.

3. Wash and pick through the cranberries. Discard any squishy or discolored berries. Stir the pie-worthy cranberries into the batter. Stir in the nuts. Pour the filling into the tart pan, slide it onto a baking sheet, and put it into the oven. Bake for 40 to 45 minutes, until the filling is set. If made in a pie plate, it will take longer to set. Let cool before removing from the tart pan.

Breads and Popovers

Many cultures have eggy breads: The Greeks make *tsoureki*, a special sweet loaf for Easter; Germans prepare stollen; Italians bake panettone, a rich bread studded with citrus. I grew up with challah, the braided Jewish egg bread, which in many homes is first blessed and then eaten every Friday night. The smell of dough baking in the oven is a welcome transition from work and school to the more relaxed weekend. But yeast breads take time. For immediate gratification, I rely on popovers. The batter is whipped up in a blender, poured into the pan, and in under an hour, with almost no effort, you have hot popovers in your bread basket. Excellent for dinner, but also for a snack—especially if you have a bit of Lemon Curd (page 136) in the fridge to spread on the steaming popover.

Challah

A while back I worked in a bakery that made challah. A few customers bought braided loaves for their Sabbath meals. Many more bought the loaves that we fashioned into adorable bears. Challah is a very easy dough to shape, and the egg glaze gives it a mahogany-like finish. Baked loaves freeze well, but, better yet, turn the leftovers into French toast or bread pudding. Even if you don't have a Sabbath tradition, this bread is worth baking.

This recipe uses instant yeast, which does not require proofing (being dissolved in warm water). Also note that this recipe uses bread flour, which is sometimes labeled "bread machine flour." Its higher gluten content gives the bread more lift and structure.

Makes 2 loaves

4 teaspoons (2 envelopes) instant yeast

7 to 8 cups bread flour

2 teaspoons kosher salt

½ cup granulated sugar

1¾ cups plus 1 teaspoon water

3 large eggs

⅓ cup vegetable oil

1 egg yolk

1. This recipe can be made in a stand mixer or by hand. In either case, in a large mixing bowl, thoroughly combine the yeast, water, 1 cup of the flour, the salt, and sugar.

2. Add 1 cup of the remaining flour at a time, continually stirring, until a sticky dough forms. Flour varies, but this step will usually take about 6 cups. If using a stand mixer, use the dough hook on low speed. If stirring by hand, use a wooden spoon. Once the dough forms, if mixing by hand, turn out onto a generously floured surface. If using a mixer, leave in the bowl.

3. Continue to add flour, about ¼ cup at a time. If doing this by hand, knead the dough using the heels of your hands. If using the mixer, continue to use the dough hook on low speed. Once the dough becomes smooth and shiny and it bounces back to the touch, it is ready for the next step.

4. Put the dough in a covered bowl (I use a large plastic tub with a lid) and let it rest in a warm place until doubled in bulk. This will take anywhere from 1 to 2 hours depending on the room's temperature. Don't rush it.

5. Punch down the risen dough and, if sticky, dust with flour so that it can be handled. Put on a floured surface and knead briefly, until smooth. Divide in half and then divide each half into thirds.

Continued on next page

Continued from previous page

As they do in professional bakeries, I use a scale to do this, because strands of equal size produce a braided loaf that rises evenly and looks beautiful.

6. Roll each portion into a strand about 12 inches long. Line a large baking sheet with parchment paper.

7. Take 3 of the strands and pinch the ends together. Braid them, and then pinch the other ends together. Tuck the pinched ends under the loaf and place on the parchment. Repeat with the second loaf. Both should fit on the baking sheet. Give the loaves room to rise and spread.

8. Mix the egg yolk with the remaining 1 teaspoon water to make an egg wash. Paint the loaves with the wash using a pastry brush. Let rise until about double in size, about 1 hour.

9. Meanwhile, preheat the oven to 350°F. Just prior to baking, brush the loaves again with the egg wash. Bake for 30 to 40 minutes, until golden brown.

Weekend French Toast

The last thing I want to do when I have a houseful of guests on a Sunday morning is stand over a griddle while they're all enjoying themselves. This French toast is the solution. Soak the bread in the batter overnight and then bake it in the oven when everyone wakes up. Not only is it a cinch to make, but the cleanup is easy, too! Serve with warm maple syrup. Or, for a special topping, gently simmer blueberries and maple syrup, and then push through a fine-mesh sieve to remove the blueberry skins.

Makes 5 servings

One 1-pound loaf sturdy white bread or challah (unsliced)

6 large eggs

1 cup 1% milk

2 tablespoons maple syrup (preferably Grade B)

½ teaspoon vanilla extract

¼ teaspoon kosher salt

¼ teaspoon ground nutmeg

Nonstick cooking spray

1. Cut the bread into about ten ¾-inch-thick slices.

2. Using a whisk, combine the eggs, milk, maple syrup, vanilla, salt, and nutmeg.

3. Dip each slice of bread in the batter. Place in a flat-bottomed storage dish, stacked up to 3 slices high. Pour the remaining batter over the slices. Cover and refrigerate overnight.

4. Preheat the oven to 400°F. Coat two baking sheets with non-stick cooking spray. Using a flat spatula, carefully lift the bread out of the storage dish and place the slices on the baking sheets in a single layer. Leave space between the slices.

5. Bake for 6 minutes. Turn over. Bake for 6 to 8 minutes more, until the egg batter is thoroughly set.

Popovers

Do you love fresh, warm bread at dinner but shy away from making it because it seems too difficult and fussy to do? If so, this recipe will get you baking. All you need is a blender and a muffin pan. Made in muffin pans, the popovers rise up light and airy, but if you want impressive height, you'll have to invest in a proper popover pan.

Makes 6 to 8 popovers

Nonstick cooking spray

3 large eggs

1¼ cups all-purpose flour

1 cup 1% milk

½ teaspoon kosher salt

1 tablespoon butter, melted

1. Preheat the oven to 400°F. Coat a muffin or popover pan with nonstick cooking spray.

2. Put the eggs, flour, milk, and salt into a blender and mix until frothy. Add the butter and blend for a few more seconds, until combined.

3. Pour the batter into the tin, filling not quite to the rim.

4. Bake for 30 to 40 minutes (depending on the size of the pan), until browned.

Toad in the Hole

This is British comfort food. It's incredibly easy to make and so satisfying to see coming out of the oven all puffed up and browned. The sausage that you use determines much of the flavor. I'm very fussy about the meat I buy. The only pork sausage that I purchase comes from a local farmer who keeps pastured pigs. I use organic chicken sausage when the farmer is out of stock.

Makes 4 large servings

2 large eggs

1 cup all-purpose flour

1 cup low-fat milk

¼ teaspoon salt

1 to 2 tablespoons vegetable oil

1 medium red onion, sliced

1 pound sausage of your choice

1 long sprig fresh rosemary

1. Whisk together the eggs, flour, milk, and salt. Refrigerate while cooking the sausage and onions.

2. Preheat the oven to 425°F. If using uncooked pork sausage, put 1 tablespoon oil in a 9-inch square baking dish (2½-quart casserole). If using a drier, precooked chicken sausage, use 2 tablespoons oil. Distribute the onions in the dish and add the sausage. Bake until browned, turning several times (large pork links will take 20 minutes total).

3. Carefully remove the pan from the oven (the fat might splatter) and pour in the batter. Lay the rosemary on top. Return to the oven.

4. Bake until browned and puffed up, 25 to 30 minutes. Like a popover, this will collapse. It's best served immediately, although leftovers are very good reheated for breakfast.

Cinnamon Sugar Puffed Pancake

Also known as a Dutch baby pancake or a German pancake, this is rich and sweet. The batter rises in the oven like a popover. It looks especially impressive when made in a well-seasoned cast-iron skillet, which can go from the oven to the table. The pancake will begin to deflate as soon as it comes out of the oven, but that is part of its drama and charm.

Makes 2 large servings

2 large eggs

¼ cup granulated sugar

⅓ cup whole milk

½ cup all-purpose flour

1 tablespoon unsalted butter

¼ teaspoon ground cinnamon

1½ teaspoons confectioners' sugar

1. Preheat the oven to 400°F.

2. Whisk the eggs and granulated sugar together. Pour in the milk and continue to whisk. Sift the flour over the mixture and whisk again until smooth. Let the batter sit for 5 minutes.

3. Heat the butter in a 10-inch ovenproof skillet over medium heat. Pour in the batter and cook for 3 minutes.

4. Transfer the skillet to the center of the oven. Bake for 14 minutes, until the edges begin to brown and the center puffs up.

5. Carefully (the pan will be hot!) remove the skillet from the oven. Immediately sift the cinnamon and confectioners' sugar over the pancake.

Cakes and Cookies

Eggs play so many roles in cooking, which is made even more clear in their myriad uses in the baking of sweets. Eggs bind and hold ingredients together. In fact, biscotti have no fat or liquid added other than eggs! Eggs can lighten batters, sometimes to astounding heights—just look at how tall and airy angel food cake is, all because of whipped egg whites. Eggs can mellow out and meld flavors, as seen in Orange and Almond Pound Cake (page 183), which would be too sharply citrusy without the yolks. All eggs are good for baking, but when you work with farmstead eggs, you get the additional nuances of their rich flavor and fresh texture. A carton of eggs from my hens in my refrigerator calls out to me to get into the kitchen and bake.

Angel Food Cake with Raspberry Sauce

If you've only tasted angel food cake purchased from a supermarket, this recipe will be a revelation. Unlike commercial angel food cakes, which often taste metallic and too sweet, this one has a clean flavor. Pour on the raspberry sauce, and you have a gorgeous finale to any meal.

When a recipe calls for this many egg whites, I measure out the volume instead of counting the eggs. Egg size depends on who is laying and the time of year (the first eggs of spring are smaller). If I specified a set number of "large eggs," I could be off by ¼ cup whites, which would make a huge difference in this cake. Angel food cake uses the same skills needed for meringues (page 145); in fact it's basically a meringue with flour added.

Makes 10 servings

FOR THE CAKE:

1¼ cups egg whites (8 to 10 whites)

½ teaspoon cream of tartar

¼ teaspoon kosher salt

1 teaspoon vanilla extract

1 cup granulated sugar

1 cup cake or pastry flour (sifted before measuring)

FOR THE RASPBERRY SAUCE:

2 cups frozen raspberries

¼ cup light brown sugar

2 teaspoons raspberry liqueur

FOR THE GARNISH:

2 cups fresh raspberries

1. Preheat the oven to 325°F with a rack in the bottom third.

2. To make the cake, in a large, clean, dry bowl with an electric mixer, beat the egg whites and cream of tartar until soft peaks form. Add the salt and vanilla. (This is easiest to do in a stand mixer, but a handheld electric mixer can be used. The whites will greatly increase in volume, so use the largest bowl you have.)

3. With the mixer running at high speed, add the granulated sugar in a slow, steady stream. Beat until stiff, shiny peaks form. (The tips of the peaks will remain upright and not fall over.)

4. This is one of the few recipes where I sift the flour before measuring. It is very important that you have exactly the right amount of flour and that it is fluffy and free of lumps. Fold ¼ cup of the flour into the egg whites. Continue to add small amounts of flour until all of it has been added and distributed evenly throughout the batter.

5. Spoon the mixture into an ungreased 10-inch angel food cake pan. Using a rubber spatula, smooth out the surface.

6. Bake for 35 to 40 minutes, until a toothpick inserted in the center of the cake comes out clean.

7. Put the cake pan upside down on a wire rack and let cool completely.

Continued on next page

Continued from previous page

8. Meanwhile, make the raspberry sauce. Put the frozen raspberries, brown sugar, and liqueur in a small saucepan over low heat and cook until the raspberries soften and burst. (Don't use the microwave for this.)

9. Strain the sauce through a fine-mesh sieve and discard the seeds.

10. When the cake is cool, run a flexible spatula along the sides of the pan to release the cake. Place the cake on a serving plate. Pour the sauce slowly over the top, letting some drip over the sides. Arrange the fresh berries on and beside the cake. Slice with a serrated knife or an angel food cake cutter.

Cocoa Angel Food Cake with Chocolate-Espresso Glaze

This cake has a hint of cinnamon. The glaze is smooth, luscious, and dark in contrast to the airy texture of the cake. All in all, it is a lovely combination.

Makes 10 servings

FOR THE CAKE:

¾ cup pastry or cake flour
  (sifted before measuring)

¼ cup unsweetened cocoa powder

¼ teaspoon kosher salt

½ teaspoon ground cinnamon

1¼ cups egg whites (8 to 10 whites)

½ teaspoon cream of tartar

1 teaspoon vanilla extract

1 cup granulated sugar

FOR THE GLAZE:

6 ounces bittersweet or
  semisweet chocolate

⅔ cup heavy cream

3 tablespoons light corn syrup

½ teaspoon instant espresso powder

¼ teaspoon ground cinnamon

1. Preheat the oven to 325°F with a rack in the bottom third.

2. To make the cake, put the flour in a bowl. Sift in the cocoa powder, salt, and cinnamon. Stir until a uniform color.

3. In a large, clean, dry bowl with an electric mixer, beat the egg whites and cream of tartar until foamy. Add the vanilla.

4. With the mixer running at high speed, add the sugar in a slow, steady stream. Beat until stiff, shiny peaks form.

5. Fold ¼ cup of the flour-cocoa mixture into the egg whites. Continue to add small amounts until all the flour is blended into the batter. Fold gently to combine.

6. Spoon the mixture into an ungreased 10-inch angel food cake pan. Using a rubber spatula, smooth the surface.

7. Bake for 35 to 40 minutes, until a toothpick inserted in the center of the cake comes out clean.

8. Put the cake pan upside down on a wire rack and let cool completely.

9. Meanwhile, make the glaze. Chop the chocolate into small pieces. Place the chocolate and the cream, corn syrup, espresso powder, and cinnamon in a small pot and heat gently until the chocolate melts, stirring frequently. Bring to a simmer and then immediately remove from the heat. Let it cool to room temperature.

10. When the cake is cool, run a flexible spatula along the sides of the pan to release the cake. Place the cake on a serving plate. Pour the sauce slowly over the top and sides. Use a spatula to coat all of the cake with the glaze. Slice with a serrated knife.

Orange and Almond Pound Cake

This is a classic pound cake in that eggs are the only leavener. As you beat the eggs into the batter, they create lift and the perfect crumb. I buy sliced almonds with the skins on, but you can use skinless almonds, too, or leave off the glaze and the nuts; that's how my sons like it. With or without glaze and/or nuts, the cake looks beautiful and tastes just the way a pound cake should.

Makes 12 servings

FOR THE CAKE:

Nonstick cooking spray

1 cup (2 sticks) unsalted butter, softened

3 cups granulated sugar

6 large eggs

3 cups all-purpose flour, sifted

1 cup sour cream (not low-fat)

1 teaspoon vanilla extract

1 teaspoon almond extract

2 teaspoons grated orange zest

FOR THE GLAZE:

1 cup confectioners' sugar

1 tablespoon orange juice, strained

1 tablespoon hot water

3 tablespoons sliced almonds, toasted

1. Preheat the oven to 350°F. Coat a 10- to 12-cup Bundt pan with nonstick cooking spray.

2. To make the cake, in a large bowl with an electric mixer, beat the butter with the granulated sugar until the texture is fluffy.

3. Add the eggs to the mixing bowl one at a time, beating thoroughly after each addition.

4. Add one-third of the flour to the mixing bowl and beat. Add one-third of the sour cream and beat. Continue in this way until all the flour and sour cream have been smoothly combined into the batter.

5. Stir in the vanilla and almond extracts and the orange zest. Note that one orange yields about 1 tablespoon of grated orange zest, which is the finely grated outer orange peel. Avoid using the white pith beneath, which is bitter. Once the zest is removed, squeeze the juice out of the orange and reserve it for the glaze.

6. Pour the batter into the Bundt pan and place it in the center of the oven. Bake about 1 hour, or until a toothpick comes out clean.

7. Let the cake cool in the pan on a wire rack. Remove the cake from the pan and place it on a sheet of aluminum foil.

8. To make the glaze, using an electric mixer, beat the confectioners' sugar, orange juice, and hot water until the glaze is shiny and smooth. Immediately pour the glaze over the cake, letting it drip down the sides. Dust with the almonds, which will stick to the glaze. When the glaze is set, transfer the cake to a serving plate.

Pistachio – Apricot Biscotti

The only fat in this biscotti batter comes from the egg yolks. Without the eggs, these cookies would be hard and dry. The yolks also contribute a deep yellow color to the batter, and the green pistachios and orange apricots add colorful highlights.

Makes 16 cookies

1 cup shelled, unsalted pistachios

3 cups all-purpose flour

1½ cups granulated sugar

¼ teaspoon kosher salt

1 teaspoon baking powder

¾ cup coarsely chopped
  dried apricots

5 large eggs

1 teaspoon vanilla extract

1. Preheat the oven to 300°F. Line two baking sheets with parchment paper.

2. Put the pistachios on another rimmed baking sheet and toast in the oven for about 10 minutes, or until they begin to change color but not darken. Let cool.

3. In a large bowl, stir together the flour, sugar, salt, and baking powder. Using your fingers, separate the sticky chopped apricots and toss them in the flour until the apricots are evenly mixed throughout. Stir in the pistachios.

4. In a small bowl, whisk the eggs and vanilla until no streaks of egg whites remain. Stir this into the flour mixture. The dough will be very sticky.

5. Flour your hands and knead the dough so that it forms a rough loaf shape. Place the dough on one of the baking sheets. Shape it into a rectangle about 13 by 4 inches in size. Bake for 50 minutes.

6. Remove the biscotti loaf from the oven and let cool for 10 minutes. Then, using a serrated knife on a cutting board, cut the loaf into ½-inch-thick slices. Put the cookies, cut side down, on the baking sheets. Bake for 20 minutes. Remove from the oven, flip the cookies over, and then bake for 20 minutes more, until golden.

7. Place the cookies on wire racks to cool. Store in an airtight container for up to 2 weeks.

Recipes by Type

You can use the recipes in this book however you like, but to help you plan your meals, here is a list of the recipes by type or course.

APPETIZERS AND SOUPS

Classic Deviled Eggs

Curried Shrimp Deviled Eggs

Tea Eggs

Seasoned Salts

    Three-Pepper Salt

    Citrus Salt

    Szechuan Pepper Salt

Beef and Egg Piroshki

Italian Egg Soup

Spanish Garlic Soup

Egg Drop Soup

Avgolemono Soup

MAIN DISHES

Egg Panini

Croque Madame

Huevos Rancheros

Steak and Eggs with Shallot-Garlic Butter
   and Sweet Onions

    Shallot-Garlic Butter

Angel Hair Pasta with Fried Eggs

Asparagus with Poached Eggs and Smoked Salmon

Poached Eggs in Twice-Baked Potatoes

Eggs Poached in Marinara

Shirred Eggs with Spinach and Cream

Shirred Eggs on Polenta

Omelet (master recipe)

Smoked Trout Omelet

Potato Frittata with Fresh Herbs

Apple and Brie Omelet

Salsa and Guacamole Frittata

Zucchini and Mint Frittata

Gremolata-Ricotta Frittata

Cheesy Egg Puff with Greens Hash

Quiche (master recipe)

Quiche with Bacon and Cheese

Onion Tart

Leek and Feta Quiche

Chard and Feta Strata

Basil and Mozzarella Tian

Savory Spinach Cheesecake

Fettuccine Alfredo with Rosemary and Garlic

Spaghetti alla Carbonara

Mayonnaise-Slathered Baked Catfish

Swordfish Kabobs with Aioli

Toad in the Hole

LIGHT MAINS AND SIDES

Green Salad with Bacon and Poached Eggs

Honey Noodle Kugel

Fried Eggs and Goat Cheese

Goat Cheese and Asparagus Custards

Cheese Soufflé

Cheese Custards

Vegetable Fried Rice

Eggs and Croutons for Steamed Vegetables

Scrambled Eggs with Sausage, Cheddar,
   and Peppers

Bombay Scrambled Eggs

Matzo Brei

Birdie in a Basket

Fried Egg Breakfast Sandwich

Pickled Beets and Eggs

Egg Salad with Chives

Egg, Potato, and Tuna Salad

Dinosaur Kale and Egg Panzanella Salad

Cobb Salad

Salmon and Egg Pan Bagnat

Weekend French Toast

Cinnamon Sugar Puffed Pancake

DESSERTS

Classic Sweet Custard

Ginger Pots de Crème

Chocolate Bread Pudding

Apple Clafoutis

Vanilla Pudding

Lemon Curd

Crème Anglaise

Eggnog

Chocolate Soufflé

Chocolate-Kahlúa Volcanoes

Chocolate-Walnut Meringue Cookies

Lemon Kisses

Pavlova with Lemon Curd Whipped Cream

All-Purpose Pastry Crusts

Graham Cracker Crust

Lemon Meringue Pie

Lime Tart

Chocolate Cream Pie with Meringue Topping

Chocolate Tart

Pumpkin Cheesecake

Peach-Lemon Chiffon Pie

Cranberry-Nut Tart

Angel Food Cake with Raspberry Sauce

Cocoa Angel Food Cake with Chocolate-
  Espresso Glaze

Orange and Almond Pound Cake

Pistachio-Apricot Biscotti

BREADS

Challah

Popovers

MASTER RECIPES

Scrambled Eggs

Fried Eggs

  Sunny Side Up

  Over Easy

  Over Hard

Hard-Cooked Eggs: Two Methods (master recipe)

Soft-Cooked Eggs

Poached Eggs (master recipe)

Mayonnaise

Aioli

Index